JUN 9 1967 70

Pickup MICHIGAN STATE UNIVERSITY
1983 LIBRARY
MAR 20 2018

WITHDRAWN

7-25-57 Direct L57401

PAUL SCOFIELD
by J. C. Trewin

BY THE SAME AUTHOR

The Shakespeare Memorial Theatre (with M. C. Day)
The English Theatre
We'll Hear a Play
Drama, 1945-1950
The Theatre Since 1900
A Play To-night
The Stratford Festival (with T. C. Kemp)
Dramatists of To-day
Mr. Macready
Edith Evans
Sybil Thorndike
Theatre Programme (Editor)
Verse Drama Since 1800 : An Essay
Plays of the Year, 13 vols. (Editor)
The Year's Work in the Theatre, 3 vols. (Editor)
    Etc.

Up From The Lizard
Down To The Lion
Printer to the House (with E. M. King)
The Story of Stratford-upon-Avon
    Etc.

Angus McBean

THEATRE WORLD MONOGRAPH No. 6

Paul Scofield

by

J. C. TREWIN

An illustrated study of his work, with a
list of his appearances on stage and screen

SALISBURY SQUARE LONDON

FOR WENDY

Theatre World Monographs

GENERAL EDITOR : FRANCES STEPHENS
CONSULTANT AND PICTURE EDITORS :
RAYMOND MANDER AND JOE MITCHENSON

COPYRIGHT 1956
by ROCKLIFF PUBLISHING CORPORATION

Printed in Great Britain
at the BURLEIGH PRESS, *Lewins Mead*, BRISTOL

CONTENTS

ACKNOWLEDGMENTS

The Author thanks Paul Scofield and Joy Parker (Mrs. Scofield) for their unremitting kindness and patience ; his wife for her constant aid ; Raymond Mander and Joe Mitchenson for expert guidance ; Nancy Burman, of the Birmingham Repertory Theatre ; and all from whom he has quoted.

The Editors thank Paul Scofield for his ready co-operation and for lending early photographs ; Tom English for ransacking the files of the Birmingham Repertory Theatre to provide pictures ; and John Goodwin for similar service at the Shakespeare Memorial Theatre, Stratford-upon-Avon.

ILLUSTRATIONS

PAUL SCOFIELD

I HEARD THE VOICE on a glum mid-October afternoon in 1945. On the previous night I had met Sean O'Casey's villagers of Clune na Geera as they made " gold embroidery out o' dancin' words " in the " wayward comedy " of *Purple Dust* at the Playhouse, Liverpool. Exhilaration and the gold-dusted phrase had melted next morning into a mist like wet fur. By the time I had travelled to Birmingham, submerged that day beneath a damp, smoky drift, the wisest thing seemed to be to fall under a train. But the thought of the Birmingham Repertory buoyed me as it would have done anybody nursed in the atmosphere of " rep ". Sir Barry Jackson's theatre had been a star-borne legend, Hy-Brasil itself. When the curtain rose upon the chronicle of *King John* (more high words) I had ceased to bother about the murk of Station Street.

The producer was Peter Brook, then twenty years old. I had missed his *Doctor Faustus* in London on the 'bus-ticket stage of the Torch Theatre (much like the upper deck of an omnibus forever traffic-jammed off Knightsbridge). Still, his ordering of Cocteau's *The Infernal Machine* on the tea-tray of the Chanticleer in Kensington had shown that he was not the kind of man to fret round the sofa, loiter by the french windows. Here now at Birmingham, *King John,* which opens as a rule with a tableau in uneasy wax, began with what resembled a Court bacchanal, all a gimble and a gyre. Presently Philip Faulconbridge, the Bastard, entered, and intuitively I knew that we were in the presence of an actor, one whose name had already got about : he had annexed playgoing Birmingham. The young man was tall and spare ; his face this afternoon had a set curiously Elizabethan as though it looked at us from a miniature by Isaac Oliver. Paul Scofield's face is no blank canvas for an actor's grease-painting. It is moulded strongly. One might feel indeed that, whatever the part and the mask, the face must remain revealingly Scofield : those high cheekbones, the forehead deep-lined beneath thick curling hair, the eyes dark under burdened brows, a tense nobility of profile. Hard to disguise—and yet critics, at times widely differing, have been moved to speak of an Elizabethan head, of " the very face and figure of an Angevin stone king in a mediæval cathedral", of the "strange tragic repose of the sculptured Renaissance *condottieri*", and of a Velasquez figure transferred from canvas to " eroded marble".

The analogies are often sculptural ; certainly it is a head to be fixed in marble or bronze. But I am thinking here of the ease with which the actor alters personality, age, period. He is never " always Scofield ". In *King John* the face that gazed at us from the Repertory stage was that of the Bastard—a man who, though he came from the " troublesome reign", was an Elizabethan out of time. The voice we heard in the " Commodity " speech (Peter Brook, a decision almost unnoticed, had altered the word to " expediency ") has become one of the most idiosyncratic on the stage. That day, and especially when bringing down the curtain with a royal patriotic brag, it seemed too light for the Bastard, for the beacon of gallantry and common sense, heart (not head) of oak. But the actor levelled at the verse so truly and, at the same time, with so much clarity—every syllable revealed, as it were, under a searching northern light—that we did not ask if he had in fact the fullest rhetorical ring of Cœur-de-Lion's son. To-day the voice, as taut or as huskily caressing as of old, has strengthened to odd splendour : to a mountain voice, rifted, chasmed, that can glitter on the peak and fall, sombre, in the sudden crevasse. It has what a poet called long ago " the random music of the turning world".

II

THE performance in *King John* lingered with me ; the extraordinary personal magnetism, the loping stride, eyes in which one could trace the growing thought, vocal gusts that almost startled the speaker. Paul Scofield, then twenty-three, had not done much Shakespeare before. Even so, it was in Shakespeare that his career began—when he was only thirteen and at Varndean School, Brighton. He was born at Hurstpierpoint, not far off, on January 21, 1922 ; his father was headmaster of the village school, and the family tree had no actor on its branches. Yet, after a short time at Varndean, where

1935 School Production: Juliet in *Romeo and Juliet,* with J. C. Gladman (Romeo)

1940 Repertory Theatre, Bideford : Dan in *Night Must Fall*

Lisel Haas

1942 Repertory Theatre, Birmingham (Travelling Repertory Theatre) : Stephen Undershaft (left) in *Major Barbara*, with W. E. Holloway (Andrew Undershaft), Margaret Leighton (Sarah Undershaft), Lee Fox (Charles Lomax), Daphne Newton (Lady Britomart Undershaft), Anthony Davies (Bilton), Margaretta Scott (Barbara Undershaft), and Basil C. Langton (Adolphus Cusins)

Herbert Paul

1942 Repertory Theatre, Birmingham (Travelling Repertory Theatre):
Horatio in *Hamlet*, with Basil C. Langton (Hamlet)

Alexander Bender

1944 Theatre Royal, Bristol (Travelling Repertory Theatre): Tybalt in
Romeo and Juliet, with Basil C. Langton (Romeo) and William Roderick
(Mercutio)

John Vickeas

1943   Whitehall Theatre : Alex Morden in *The Moon is Down*, with Lewis
Casson (Mayor Orden)

Lisel Haas

1943 C.E.M.A. Tour (Travelling Repertory Theatre) : Donald in *Three-Cornered Moon*, with Joy Parker (Elizabeth Rimplegar)

he says he was not noticeably an infant phenomenon, he was acting away at pressure. The part ? Surprisingly to us now, Juliet, in a play that he has since got to know rather well. A picture survives of this Juliet, uncontrollably mischievous and framed in plaits. Presently he was off the balcony, and in the Forest of Arden to play Rosalind, again in plaits—singularly fetching thick Nordic ones. In 1938, when his voice had broken (it is not mended yet), he was Hal in *Henry the Fourth, Part One,* Eastcheap's good companion and paladin of " Nor can our England brook a double reign of Harry Percy and the Prince of Wales".

It was quite clear from these first school-hall adventures, this mixture of greasepaint and chalk-dust, that he would go permanently to the stage. It was not just a schoolboy talent, something to be puzzled over years later by a bank manager in the West Riding (ex-Lady Macbeth) or an oil engineer by the Persian Gulf (ex-Shylock and a shot at Petruchio). Paul Scofield keeps still, as a mascot, a cudgel that he waved when he went up at the age of thirteen, to act at the Theatre Royal, Brighton. Sir John Martin-Harvey wanted supers in a crowd scene of *The Only Way,* and no one shouted louder than Scofield. That was in 1935. Four years later he began his only way—as a student at the school linked in those days with the Croydon Repertory Theatre : I have no doubt that if they had done *Romeo*—and they did not—he would have been Potpan or Friar John.

War came, Croydon closed down, and Paul Scofield went on to the school (run by John Fernald) attached to the London Mask Theatre at the Westminster. Students could get small-part experience in the Mask productions, and it was at the Westminster, upon April 16, 1940, that Scofield spoke his first lines on the professional stage—not very exciting lines—as the Third Clerk (" Yes, sir ") and the First Soldier (" Yes, sir ") in Drinkwater's *Abraham Lincoln* : Stephen Murray as Lincoln. He had during the season walking-on parts—less teasing to the memory—in *Desire Under the Elms* and Priestley's *Cornelius.*

The young man was now at home backstage : more so, he may have felt wryly, than on the stage itself : he was a good hand at painting scenery, but was this the path to Hamlet ? He doubted it. Then, " not shriving-time allowed " (as he would hear himself saying one day), and in the manner of his unlikely profession, he was thrown headlong into leading parts. It was not in London. Eileen Thorndike (Dame Sybil's younger sister) and Herbert Scott, who were both teaching at the Mask Theatre School, evacuated some of the students to Bideford in North Devon during the fierce autumn of 1940. Here in the little white town by the Torridge, Amyas Leigh's town, Paul Scofield found himself, within an evening, acting Lear, Macbeth and Petruchio, characters to which he has not since returned. They were all done during the same programme in a mosaic of Shakespeare extracts with which the Thorndike-Scott season opened at the new Bideford Repertory Theatre, staffed entirely by students. A fine chance if you did not object to work. Scofield has never objected. He became a local star in that withdrawn world of North Devon, one which had no idea that in years ahead it would hold a Festival of its own and look wonderingly at Brecht and Ronald Duncan.

The Bideford plays were varied. Paul Scofield spent the winter now carrying about a head in a hatbox—this fellow, "Danny", of *Night Must Fall,* had a sulky bravado—now doing a little steady blackmail (*Ladies in Retirement*), talking in clipped Morse with a flapper of the period (*Hay Fever*), or being alertly romantic on the *Granite* of Lundy (there, for a Bideford audience, was something like local colour). In a play of less serious intention he observed with some feeling, " If you're a greyhound I'm Fred Astaire." A pity, I feel, that no photograph exists of that double act in *Red Peppers.* A key to these parts is in a list at the end of this book. It is enough to say that, at Bideford during that toiling season, Paul Scofield knew what the life of a repertory actor was like[1]; not, as it is often assumed, a sentence on the treadmill. In true " rep ", quick forge and working-house of thought, mind is sharpened against mind, enthusiasm matched with enthusiasm.

From Bideford during 1941 Eileen Thorndike moved her company to Cambridge and to a production of Obey's *Noah* : Paul Scofield heavily disguised as the loquacious ancient of days. When, after this, the students disbanded, he went in July to London. As so many young players had done—and as they continue to do—he

---

[1] The repertory actor earns
My very high respect,
For think of all the parts he learns
And has to recollect . . .

Guy Boas.

sought out Robert Atkins. Scofield found that re-born Elizabethan
at lunch in a public-house near the Palace Theatre. He was re-
hearsing the war's second revival of *Chu-Chin-Chow,* but—more
important from Scofield's point of view—he was also casting an
E.N.S.A. tour of *The Taming of the Shrew.* It was a lucky meeting.
Atkins engaged this urgent youth—who seemed both to use
seven-league boots and to walk as delicately as Agag—for the fifty-
odd lines of the veteran Vincentio. Later he rose to Tranio ; in
the *Shrew* it can be promotion to go from master to man. Early
in 1942 it would have been a step from this tour to the Messenger
in *Medea* which Dame Sybil Thorndike and Sir Lewis Casson were to
take on a round of the village halls of mining Wales. As if it were
not enough to come for the first time under so wisely exacting a
director as Sir Lewis, Scofield went suddenly sick after a few
rehearsals ; this episode in his career ended at—of all places—a
military hospital in the Welsh hills, at Bettws-y-Coed.

   To-day, if you ask the tour manager, Mrs. Clark, the Old Vic's
loved " Clarkie", about Paul Scofield, she will reply in one sad
word : "Mumps". He was a marked man. You cannot have
mumps before a Greek tragedy. " The idea", as Lady Bracknell
might have said, " is grotesque and irreligious. I will not hear of
such excesses."

III

GLOOMILY, once out of quarantine, Scofield, returned to
London. In the enforced sociability of a theatre agent's lift he met
a manager, and this plutocrat, without flinching at the tale of
mumps, promptly engaged him. Agreed, his part, the Hotel Clerk
in a tour of the buttermilk comedy of *Jeannie,* could hardly have been
less ambitious ; it has left no dint on the records. Presently he
was able to go over to the Mallowhurst prefect Ainger, "nearing
nineteen, good-looking, and athletic ", in a touring revival of
Young Woodley which had cropped up unexpectedly in the war-time
theatre.[1] Geoffrey Hibbert was Woodley to whom he had to say,
" Look here, kid, for the thousandth time, what's the trouble ? "

[1] *Jeannie* was sent out by A.R.P. Productions; *Young Woodley* by John Corfield.

At this period of sixes-and-sevens touring companies would use the hallowed stage of the Birmingham Repertory, and in June 1942 Paul Scofield looked with natural eagerness into that sharply-raked auditorium in Station Street. Basil C. Langton's company, the T. R. T., or Touring Repertory Theatre, which had leased the " Rep", was then working in the Birmingham parks. Langton, an actor with a lot of classical experience—he was a Stratford Hamlet in 1940—met Scofield and invited him to play Horatio for the T.R.T. Soon afterwards the young man, as a permanent member of Langton's company, stood again on the Birmingham Repertory stage that he would get to know uncommonly well. Horatio was the part he enjoyed most. He remembers the production especially because Joy Parker, a London-born actress four years younger, who had been a repertory student at Birmingham, was back there to play an Ophelia of gentle, bewildered pathos : no reeling, writhing, and fainting in coils. Midland people think still of Scofield's Horatio, faithfulness incarnate, a man fit, as not all Horatios are, to be held in Hamlet's heart of heart.[1]

He went on with Langton to an Arts Council munition-hostel tour of *Arms and the Man,* acted wherever it was possible to find or improvise a stage. He was Sergius Saranoff, that Neapolitan-ice hussar, operatic paladin, whose hand is more accustomed to the sword than to the pen—he says so himself—and Joy Parker was Louka, the Bulgarian maid. Scofield, a realist, did not entirely enjoy these " pomping " tours, too easily romanticised, though he appreciated the value they had in keeping a hard-pressed theatre alive in the provinces. When *Arms and the Man* ended he and Joy Parker were both engaged for Langton's production of *The Moon Is Down* at the Whitehall Theatre, London, a fierce little play by John Steinbeck about the Nazi occupation of Norway : he had a small part and Joy an understudy. It mattered more to them that between the pre-London tour and the Whitehall opening they were married. In *The Moon Is Down* Scofield, without mumps, found himself acting with Lewis Casson at last. The play did not run long, and it hardly seemed that his luck held : he got a job at what was supposed then to be the practically immortal " Q " Theatre, Kew Bridge—closed in 1956 after thirty years of professional life—

[1] *Hamlet*, in full text, was performed in two parts. A first performance took it to the end of the play scene ; at a second came the rest of the tragedy, with the play scene repeated as prologue.

Lisel Haas

1944   Repertory Theatre, Birmingham : Prince Po in *The Circle of Chalk*, with
Mary Kimber (Chang-Hi-Tang)

Lisel Haas

1944   Repertory Theatre, Birmingham. The Clown (left) in *The Winter's
Tale*, with Gwen Nelson (Mopsa), Billy Tasker (Autolycus) and Monica
Stutfield (Dorcas)

Lisel Haas

1944 Repertory Theatre, Birmingham : William d'Albini (centre) in *The Empress Maud*, with Gwen Nelson (Adelicia of Louvain) Eileen Beldon (Maud), George Skillan (Henry of Blois) and Michael Madell (Robert, Earl of Gloucester)

Lisel Haas

1944 Repertory Theatre, Birmingham : Toad in *Toad of Toad Hall*, with Jack Rodney (Mole), Duncan Ross (Water Rat) and Peter Streuli (Badger)

Lisel Haas

1945 Repertory Theatre, Birmingham : Valentine in *Doctor's Delight*, with Wilfrid Walter (Crank), Monica Stutfield (Angelica), Jack Rodney (Thomas Douche), Gwen Nelson (Toinette) and Peter Streuli (Dr. Douche)

Lisel Haas

1945 Repertory Theatre, Birmingham : A Fisherman (second from right) in *Land's End*, with Scott Sunderland (Hugh Gifford), Gwen Nelson (Judith), Monica Stutfield (Valentine Galbraith), Mabel France (Mrs. Newsome) and John Harrison (Vernon)

Lisel Haas

1945   Repertory Theatre, Birmingham : Constantin in *The Seagull*, with
Julia Lang (Nina)

Lisel Haas

1945   Repertory Theatre, Birmingham : Faulconbridge in *King John*, with Mabel
France (Elinor), David Read (King John) and Denis Quilley (Robert)

Lisel Haas

1945   Repertory Theatre, Birmingham : Jerry Devine in *Juno and the Paycock*, with Julia Lang (Mary Boyle)

Lisel Haas

1945　Repertory Theatre, Birmingham : John Tanner in *Man and Superman*, with Herbert Vanderfelt (Roebuck Ramsden)

Lisel Haas

1945   Repertory Theatre, Birmingham : Dr. Wangel in *The Lady from the Sea,* with Duncan Ross (A Stranger) and Eileen Beldon (Ellida Wangel)

1945   Repertory Theatre, Birmingham : A Crusader in *1066 and All That,* with Lysbeth Harley (Crusader's Wife), Margaret Oak (Constance), and Jennifer Maddox (Blanche)

Thomas Holte

1946 Memorial Theatre, Stratford-upon-Avon : Cloten in *Cymbeline*

and was, alas, sacked during rehearsal. Never mind : back to the
munition hostels with Langton. On this tour he and Joy Parker
had parts in a very American snippet of a comedy called *Three-
Cornered Moon*, about a Brooklyn family facing a financial loss which
makes the three sons and a daughter dash out to get work. Scofield
played an egotistical author. Passable fun ; but nothing to
remember. A Christmas season brought them to the Theatre
Royal, Bristol, not long re-opened, the gold and green jewel-case,
down among the warehouses, that had held so much since Garrick's
day. Here, in " our oldest theatre and our newest", the Langton
company put on three plays including *Romeo and Juliet* (Scofield,
very much an old hand in this tragedy, as a Tybalt with all the
pouncing venom of the King of Cats). From the gallant make-do
of war-shattered Bristol the company went again to the munition
hostels. Scofield had turned to Oliver Farrant, decisive and
slightly donnish, " something of the boy left in him and something
of the intellectual man", in Priestley's aptly-named *I Have Been Here
Before*. At last, in the autumn of 1944, surcease from touring.
The city was Birmingham : Scofield had been there before as well,
and there now his fortune would begin. He was in his twenty-
third year and a member of Sir Barry Jackson's company at the
" Rep", something that in the English theatre is equivalent to
winning a Blue.

Birmingham recalls Scofield at that time as an actor of what
someone described as shaggy grace. He was a lyrical-romantic
actor. He had also a gift for the ironic, the sardonic, the quizzical.
He could not be clamped to any recognised " Scofield part", and
though his looks alone assured prosperity as a romantic juvenile,
it was clear that he could never be obvious, never move suavely in
the theatre's hugger-mugger of " lounge-hall " and " library".
From the first he could cause the sudden tingle, stir the languid air.
Birmingham knew that the stage lay open before this striding actor
with the sierra-voice of peak and valley, the tentative gestures, the
face in which pensive age and extreme youth stood for ever on
guard. So early he had the major actor's hypnotic power : he
drew his watchers into the scene as he did at once in the stylised
romance of *The Circle of Chalk*, an English version of a German
translation from the Chinese. Later, after " an angular assumption
of years " (T. C. Kemp's phrase) as Reginald in *Getting Married*,

came his first sketch of the Clown in *The Winter's Tale,* a part doomed to be squeaked or ground out by the hack Shakespearean comic, performances as wearing as a night with a rusty pump-handle. Paul Scofield saw the Clown as a broadly bucolic youth, dulcified in good humour, from Warwickshire's rural heart, Bohemia-by-Arden, the inner sheepfolds : one had never more resented the guile of Autolycus. This Clown was an endearing sheepdog : all were happy when he announced that he and his father had been gentlemen born any time these four hours. The voice had in it the warmth of the cottage kitchen, and its Scofield crackle was here the crackling of clean straw. Toad of Toad Hall (" Poop-poop ! ") arrived at Christmas, a bombastic balloon ready for the pin.

T. C. Kemp, long honoured as the *Birmingham Post's* drama critic, watched Scofield acutely : notice after notice expressed belief in the young man's future, marked his ability to work from within, observed the effect of those vocal shifts and elisions, the tangy, compelling utterance. Parts in Molière, Goldsmith, O'Casey, and Tchehov (his first Constantin) confirmed Scofield's readiness : they showed too what is less familiar in " rep", his way of lighting each part freshly, considering it from a personal angle which was rarely the usual one. It was said of him that one could trace the past of a Scofield character and that he kept the audience with him after curtain-fall. Certainly he was not " always Scofield ": Young Marlow and Constantin had only their youth in common.

Naturally he returned for the winter season of 1945. It was then he met the young director who would have much influence upon him. Peter Brook, in the sunrise of his career, looked, as he does now, like a cherub who should be gilded and blowing a long thin trumpet over a theatre proscenium. People were still saluting a boy's genius : later they would begin to ask sourly what the devil he meant by it. But Brook has not run to seed as other Infant Phenomena have. His strength has always been his imaginative independence. He never saw the productions that old hands compare with his ; always he has taken his own line. It was fresh daybreak when he and Scofield got together at Birmingham in a raid upon *Man and Superman*, a production accused of excessive quietism. It did for once permit listeners to observe the structure of the thought : Scofield, as Tanner, divided those eloquent cascade-speeches into their glittering filaments. The method did not come off invariably : there were passages when charm had to hide a gap. Even so, many listeners had not heard the play more lucidly expounded. *King John* (where we came in) was next. After this Brook turned to Ibsen and *The Lady From The Sea* where he experimented with one of the " Brook pauses " that could foreshadow eternity. Doctor Wangel ("In many respects I seem to be standing between fire and water ") seemed to worry Scofield, prim in moustache and frock-coat : a Birmingham critic said unkindly that he resembled the late Doctor Crippen. No matter : it had been a powerful autumn. Birmingham hardly knew whether to be pleased or sorry when it learned that Sir Barry Jackson had become Director of the Shakespeare Memorial Theatre at Stratford-upon-Avon, and that Paul Scofield was crossing to the Festival of 1946.

IV

SCOFIELD was lucky to go to Stratford in that serene spring of 1946. Externally, the town looked much as usual : the Avon, swan-feathered, drawing a silver bow beside it from the bridges to Holy Trinity ; lime-buds rosy in the church avenue ; blossom fragile above plum-brick and russet walls ; elms newly green at Charlecote of the Lucies ; daisies sparkling on the way to Shottery ; the Guild Chapel phantasmal at night against Indian-ink shadow ; and the Memorial Theatre, its windows lit, set by the Avon like a moored liner. The lovable town, most genuinely itself in spring and in late autumn, had had its Shakespeare Festival of one kind or another since 1879. But 1946 would be marked in record with a white stone. This was the year after the war, everywhere a time of resurgence, fresh hope. At Stratford there was a new approach to the Festival. Sir Barry Jackson had been charged with the task of replanning, and the union of his name with the new scheme— one that would sponge away Memorial Theatre parochialism— brought the national Press to Stratford ; some critics, indeed, for the first time. Before then, except in certain places, Stratford notices had been sporadic. As Hilton Brown has said, " We are a great people for labels, and we furnish them with well-nigh imperishable gum". A tradition had grown that, at a Stratford

Festival, performances were no more than those of a moderate
" rep " : newcomers who had not troubled to go down during the
nineteen-twenties and nineteen-thirties seized upon the idea.

The truth was that there had always been notable work at
Stratford for those who cared to seek it. Agreed, it could have
been better all round, far better. Major performances had not had
the right setting, and between the wars few fashionable West End
actors made the journey. Still, those who recalled Frank Cellier,
Randle Ayrton, John Laurie, Baliol Holloway, George Hayes,
Donald Wolfit, Dorothy Green, Fabia Drake, Barbara Couper, the
young Pamela Brown, and several others, with the productions of
Bridges-Adams and the caracoling of Komisarjevsky, could not be
too destructive. (Lately old Stratfordians, old saurians, have been
heretical. Publicity has blazed, but memories stay. Was not the
standard in 1952 and 1954 below that of the years when Bridges-
Adams improvised in Greenhill Street—prehistoric, cinema-bound
years between the burning of the first Memorial and the opening
of the new ?)

That said, there is no doubt that in many ways 1946 brought a
new Stratford. Sir Barry Jackson could not be other than
inspiring : his company had a flashing eagerness, a sunrise spirit.
It was Stratford at its spring running. There were experienced
artists, Valerie Taylor, Robert Harris ; but we think first of the
young Paul Scofield, Donald Sinden (also a Sussex man and now an
admired film actor), John Harrison (who has turned his poet's
mind to production), Joy Parker, Hugh Griffith, and Myles Eason.
Chief among these was Scofield. He was not on the stage for the
first night, the gloomy première of The Tempest. The fates mocked
Stratford ; Prospero's isle remained obstinately machine-bound,
no place for any epithalamic spectacle of sounds and sweet airs.
Scofield arrived soon afterwards in a much-cut Nugent Monck
version of Cymbeline. He played the coarse-grained Cloten and
made of him something quite miraculously brainless, a walking
block, the eyes dulled, the face fixed in oafish sullen obstinacy
beneath the brush of hair. He was the last man—but Shakespeare
is to blame for this—to have ordered an aubade to his lady, and
such a nonpareil as Imogen. At one point I thought of a line from
a later dramatist, " Dost thou understand that, changeling, dangling
thy hands like bobbins before thee ? Why dost thou not stir,

Angus McBean

1946 Memorial Theatre, Stratford-upon-Avon : Don Adriano de Armado
in *Love's Labour's Lost*, with David O'Brien (Moth)

Thomas Holte

1946 Memorial Theatre, Stratford-upon-Avon : Henry in *King Henry V*.

Angus McBean

1946 Memorial Theatre, Stratford-upon-Avon : Malcolm in *Macbeth,* with
Julian Somers (Macduff)

Angus McBean

1946   Memorial Theatre, Stratford-upon-Avon : Lucio in *Measure for Measure*,
with David King-Wood (Vincentio)

puppet ? thou wooden thing upon wires ! '' Cloten '' asked for decapitation and got it '', said Eric Keown simply. Yet even this man had one moment when royalty shone : the exchange with Caius Lucius. '' Make pastime with us a day or two, or longer; if you seek us afterwards in other terms, you shall find us in our salt-water girdle.'' There Scofield's eyes gleamed : Cloten would fight.

Love's Labour's Lost which followed, produced by Peter Brook, has been named with some reason as the definitive revival of its generation. (All it lacked was the milky-mouse Nathaniel that Miles Malleson gave to London two years later.) In 1946 *Love's Labour* had come again to fashion : in a Paris revival the page Moth was being allowed to speak an epigram of Voltaire. Brook chose to set the rustle of conversation-pieces, so picked, so peregrinate, in the modes of Watteau[1] '' because the style of his dresses, with its broad, undecorated expanses of billowing satin seemed the ideal visual correlative of the essential sweet-sad mood of the play.'' A silent, chalk-pale zany attended the Princess.

The company was loyally with its producer. The lyric comedy of youth's affectations came through with the voice of '' Love, whose month is ever May''. When the Court of Love had closed, when its rallies, its conceits, its silken terms, were sped, Brook— with the aid of another daring pause—expressed piercingly that fall of frost upon the night. Mercade, entering on the rout of the Worthies, brought with his tidings of death the realities of life. Presently rustics and courtiers stood there unmoving, the blue arch of night profound behind and above them ; both masques over, both plays played, torch-fire quivering over the singers, and the world of Navarre ready to fade to air. '' You that way, we this way '', Scofield should have said in the voice of Don Adriano de Armado. Oddly, Brook gave the words to the Princess.

Armado is the fantastical Spaniard : his name derives surely from the Armada about whose defeat England would still have been talking : the galleons whose shattered remnants scudded for home by the northern and western seas. Scofield, curiously, meditatively detached from the rest of the play, managed to humanise a part that had been deemed almost unactable. He had '' tawny Spain '' in

[1] '' *Love's Labour's Lost* is . . . a Watteau . . . of charm and that significance in ordered beauty which unity alone can give, rather than a sprawling cartoon with one ear and one hand by the master, and the rest by a pupil of no particular talent.''—James Agate, *The Contemporary Theatre, 1923.*

his manner ; generations of grandees spoke in his voice. He had a charming precision and a rather weary courtesy ; in his brain a mint of phrases on which he drew in tones resolute but fragile. Somebody called him pavonine ; much better was Philip Hope-Wallace's "faintly reminiscent of an over-bred and beautiful old borzoi". We think of him now, standing melancholy, the long fingers poised about the black cane that pointed his dignity, and his face saddened by the long, thinly-falling crescents of moustache that curled from his upper lip.

After this, *Henry the Fifth,* usually a Stratford favourite, had no luck. It lost its way in production, an oddly decorous one that its director (Dorothy Green), could have enlivened and enriched. For some reason an interval with its sociable tramplings was wedged between the French and English nocturnes at Agincourt. Atmosphere, laboriously summoned, melted at once. No wonder Scofield could not find the note ; strangely, he seemed to add years to Henry (in the very May-morn of his youth), and during the familiar fanfares and orations his voice betrayed him : like that piece of uncurrent gold, it was cracked within the ring. But we knew that the man was there, waiting to be revealed. Henry came up suddenly in the reading of the battle-lists when Scofield touched the names ("Davy Gam, esquire") to a queer, memorial-tablet beauty : emotion quivered behind the simple, controlled speaking of

> O God, Thy arm was here ;
> And not to us, but to Thy arm alone,
> Ascribe we all.

Henry was not his part : we wanted the Muse of Fire. In *As You Like It,* practically a night off, he dealt with the dire elder brother, Oliver de Boys, who pairs most implausibly with Celia (it became more plausible at Stratford where the Celia was Joy Parker). Oliver has the speech about the lioness, the snake, and the wretched, ragged man. Mercifully, Scofield did not make the error of a Festival Oliver not long before, who said one night to a baffled Rosalind and Celia :

> . . . Under which bush's shade
> A *Baroness,* with udders all drawn dry,
> Lay crouching, head on ground,
> With cat-like watch.

Scofield was his true self again in *Macbeth* : the best Malcolm within memory, clear, bold, and frank, at the end like sun chasing away night. The tragedy itself, in Jacobean dress, appeared to have dwindled in scale and power, and constant roaming up and down a double staircase, and in and out of flickering curtains, impeded any tragic stride. The elemental quality was blurred. No doubt, though, about Scofield's Malcolm: his spirits shone through him: we could not believe that Macbeth was tricked by the pretence in the English scene. Earlier, in the fatal daybreak of Inverness, Scofield had shown how he could present nervous excitement without behaving, as many actors do, like a weathervane boxing the compass.

He completed his season with a Lucio in *Measure For Measure,* a fellow drily ironic and a symbol of that corrupt, licentious Vienna misgoverned by a Duke who chose to haunt it as Haroun-al-Raschid his Baghdad. Lucio's ribaldry was twanged off without hesitation. One had thought that, with the exception of Dennis Arundell thirteen years before, the best in this kind were but shadows. Now at last Lucio had grown to a personage again, a man-about-Vienna with a slippery tongue: his wife enforced would hardly complain of tedium.

So the Festival of 1946 ended with Paul Scofield at its core. He was known for his variety, his sense of the ironic and the fantastic, his loping stride that could fall to a measured progress (Armado), and the voice, sometimes wayward, sometimes flawed, that (Armado again) could be stilled to gravity, a thread glimmering in the sunlight of Navarre. He is, I think, described as he was in 1946, in a children's book,[1] gay and inventive, that Joy Parker had written and illustrated. It is dedicated to him, and we meet in it for a moment a young actor :

> " A young man came walking through
> the field this afternoon . . . He stopped and
> spoke to me . . . He was tall and his hair
> shone like new pennies in the sun. He
> walked with long strides, he was happy—
> and he sang and talked to himself".

It had been a happy season for them and for their elder child, a son, Martin (born in 1944). Joy had played Miranda, Celia, and the Maria of *Love's Labour's Lost,* one of those Watteau figures.

[1] *The Story of Benjamin Scarecrow* by Joy Parker (Heinemann, 1946).

They both came back to Stratford in 1947. Meantime, in what Sir Max Beerbohm calls "the great pale platitude of the meantime", Scofield had made one brief appearance in London, his first since *The Moon Is Down*. It was at the Arts Theatre Club in *A Phoenix Too Frequent,* Fry's frivolous epistle from the Ephesians. He was the N.C.O., who lost a body but who found a wife,[1] and Harold Hobson noticed his way of ending a phrase, on a rising note, in tones suddenly detached and meditative. I can hear yet the confidential and delightedly frank

> I was born in the hills
> Between showers, a quarter of an hour
> before milking-time.
> Do you know Pyxa ?

No one, seeing the light in the eye of Tegeus-Chromis, and hearing that eager interest, would have dared to turn away. It was another example of Scofield's ability to get on terms with his audience, to dislodge all barriers between stage and auditorium. At the Arts that night everybody knew Pyxa, the crossing of two troublesome roads, the beechwoods, the owls and doves, the cresses and kingcups, the river, and the windfallen tower of Phrasidemus.

V

THE story of Paul Scofield is that of an actor's progress. He has never lived laborious days in the gossip-column. At Stratford, as at Birmingham, and as later in London, he gained his public solely by his performances. Off-stage he slipped unobtrusively into a private life that was genuinely private. His first Stratford play in 1947 was the lyric tragedy of *Romeo and Juliet,* by now (one would have said) as much a mascot of his as the *Only Way* cudgel. This

[1] Scofield would recognise a few years later—during the life of that phoenix infrequent, *Venice Preserv'd*—Otway's version of the classic story which Christopher Fry had used in the tomb. Aquilina says in the second act :
> How could I frame my face to fit my mourning,
> With wringing hands attend him to his grave,
> Fall swooning on his hearse : take mad possession
> Even of the dismal vault where he lay buried,
> There, like the Ephesian matron, dwell, till thou,
> My lovely soldier, com'st to my deliverance ?

Angus McBean

1946　Memorial Theatre, Stratford-upon-Avon : Oliver in *As You Like It,*
with Joy Parker (Celia)

John Vicke

1946   Arts Theatre : Tegeus-Chromis in *A Phoenix Too Frequent*, with
Hermione Hannen (Dynamene)

Angus McBean

1947 Memorial Theatre, Stratford-upon-Avon : Mercutio in *Romeo and Juliet*, with John Harrison (Benvolio)

Angus McBean

1947 Memorial Theatre, Stratford-upon-Avon : Sir Andrew Aguecheek in *Twelfth Night,* with John Blatchley (Sir Toby Belch) and Dudley Jones (Feste)

time he acted Mercutio; it was by no means the kind of production
known of old. The director was the inevitable Peter Brook, and—
except during his Dali-designed version of *Salome* at Covent Garden
years ahead—he would never shock the critics so much. Looking
back, it seems to me that the outcry was exaggerated. Brook did
some perverse things ; but he could also impress himself so firmly
that it is not hard to evoke the production to-day when many later
and matter-of-course revivals are clean out of mind. Months
after *Romeo* he claimed, in a vigorous defence of his methods, that
it is " a play of wide spaces in which all scenery and decoration
easily become an irrelevance, in which one tree on a bare stage can
suggest the loneliness of a place of exile ; one wall, as in Giotto,
an entire house. Its atmosphere is described in a single line,
' These hot days is the mad blood stirring', and its treatment must
be to capture the violent passion of two children lost among the
warring fury of the Southern houses."

Opponents held that some of the scenery and decoration was
too obtrusively irrelevant, and that though Brook summoned with
fantastic skill the scorch of the Veronese noonday, he had cared
too little for the sound of the verse or for the essential plot-
mechanics (his cutting of a key scene, the Friar's " Take thou this
vial . . . and this distilled liquor drink thou off", roused academic
frenzy). Still, the production as a whole did not deserve the
unleashed thunders. Some of us do not forget the suggestion of
that cincture of crenellated city walls ; the sky's " great tent of
Mediterranean blue", an amorphous, hazy blue ; the speaking of
Chorus (John Harrison), sad and melodious, as he paced the stage
at curtain-rise and closed the play with lines snatched from the
Prince ; the first isolated meeting of the lovers, world forgot ;
and, above all, the impact of Paul Scofield's Mercutio. The part
can be vulgarised into a noisy swasher who would never have had
upon his lips the glistening aria of Queen Mab. As Scofield played
him, he was the Renaissance, flag in air. One thinks of him now,
stretched upon the stage in the torchlight, a great caped cloak flung
about him, arm raised and eyes rapt as he let the speech flower
into the silence of those grotesquely-visaged masquers. Peter
Ustinov said of Mab that Scofield spoke it as " a vague elusive
nocturne . . . It was a man who didn't like to be referred to as a
poet, talking in his sleep." He talked of dreams ; but he was not

dreaming when his steel flashed upon the Capulets ("Tybalt, you *rat-catcher!* Will you walk?"). The inflammable young Mercutio had the courtier's, soldier's, scholar's, eye, tongue, sword. At his death one knew that light ebbed from the baking noon. It was not an actor's end : a man had died. And a plague o' both your houses !

Again, this season, Scofield acted Lucio and Armado. In *The Tragical History of Doctor Faustus,* revived from 1946, he followed the Welshman, Hugh Griffith, as Mephistophilis. He spoke the verse quietly, but with diction diamond-cut : here the wayward voice was obedient. His eyes were dark with the sorrow of the damned, the spirits that fell with Lucifer. Mephistophilis, as he spoke "For where we are is hell", knew eternity and its torment, beyond any physical horrors of the brimstone-pit. It was far to a *Twelfth Night* done on the evening of Shakespeare's Birthday. After the day's wind and rain, Stratford in a world of waters, we came once more to the release of Illyria, a land poised and pavilioned against a sky luminous with summer, yet touched (we felt) with autumnal shade. There was matter for a May morning, but we were left with the sigh of "Youth's a stuff will not endure". Laughter survived in Walter Hudd's Malvolio, never a dire buffoon, and in Paul Scofield's Andrew, a wistful, pliant lack-wit, steering bewitched through the shimmering maze. "I was adored once" said Andrew, and all hearts were with the foolish fellow, a child who must not be hurt, no tinny-squeaking toy. Nothing could beat this Andrew's bravery when no enemy was near. For two or three minutes at a time he was a very devil in his own mind, a sort of Illyrian Walter Mitty. Scofield had never looked more wistful ; certainly he had never been more crumpled. Alan Dent called him "a knight made of pink blancmange". In the duel I thought of melting junket and of Hunt on Liston : "The faintness with which he sinks back on Sir Toby's breast is absolute ' dissolution and thaw '. "

He had one more part, Pericles, Prince of Tyre, in the play that had previously been known at Stratford only in a version (1900) botched by John Coleman in the grand manner. Coleman, a likeable veteran, had had *Pericles* on his mind for years. He did not hesitate "to purge the first act, to eradicate the banality of the second, to omit the irrelevant Gower chorus, and altogether to eliminate the obscenity of the fourth act." What the audience heard proved finally to be rather less like Shakespeare than *The Sign of the Cross*. In 1947 Nugent Monck, who had a name for firm cutting, if not in the Coleman style of purging and eradication, leapt at *Pericles* with sword drawn : we came out of the Memorial Theatre just a hundred minutes after curtain-rise. The entire first act had gone : not a hint of Antiochus, nothing of the " field of stars " or of the " blind mole that casts copt hills towards heaven", nothing of the misery of Tarsus once brought so sternly to Robert Atkins's grass bank in Regent's Park. The play, as we had it, opened at the beginning of Act II with Scofield's Pericles flung upon the shore of Pentapolis. What was left he acted in the high-romantic spirit and with a direct pathos : the tenderness of " A terrible childbed hast thou had, my dear " vibrates in memory. The Recognition scene suffered from a too-clenched production, but already Scofield could assume the years and the sorrow of the mature Pericles, and Daphne Slater's Marina came as an unsmutch'd lily, blossom from the rank earth of Mitylene. Scofield's completely-realised Pericles was still three years off.

Near the end of the Stratford season one heard some troubled comment on his voice : its very strangeness, its uncertain splendour, might become as much of a mannerism as an occasional harsh intake of breath or as the Olivier-pounce at a sentence's end. Nevertheless, the range of his playing astonished : with him the readiness was all, though he must have worried any admirer who sought always for the unchanging picture-postcard profile : he never looked the same twice over.

Everyone was happy at the prospect of his return home in the following spring. By now he was an honorary Stratfordian : no actor within memory had so captured the town and the Festival.

VI

BETWEEN seasons London saw his Mercutio and moonstruck Sir Andrew at His Majesty's.[1] Later he went over to Hammersmith

---

[1] *Richard the Second*, in which Scofield did not act, was also in this brief early autumn season at His Majesty's. Joy Parker, Richard's Queen, had appeared at the Festival of 1947 in the three plays, *Richard the Second*, *The Tempest* (Ariel), and *The Merchant of Venice* (Jessica) in which her husband was not cast.

and to Foppington's brother, Young Fashion, in Vanbrugh's *The Relapse* at the Lyric, a devilish smart play, stap my vitals, and unbowdlerised, but a mere framework of a part. This was only a prelude to the third Stratford season (1948). Scofield, it was announced, would alternate with Robert Helpmann in the performances of Hamlet. The Festival duly began in mid-April with *The Life and Death of King John* as they called it on the Memorial Theatre programme, letting the banners wave. Stratford playgoers could have said, in the words of the Elizabethan traveller, that "having passed the Line, they with joy recovered sight of the Starres which so long they had not seen". It was, I remember, a glittering spring day in which swans, ready on their cue, floated double, swan and shadow, upon an Avon of willowed glass : nothing like that sulky October afternoon when Scofield had played the Bastard in Birmingham. This new *King John* was a mediocre production. We think now of its symbolism of crumbling pillar and rotting flag ; of exasperating male costumes that seemed to derive from either modern battle-dress or *Miss Hook of Holland ;* of a grotesqued Austria (a part doomed to suffer in the theatre), and of some over-anxious make-up. Robert Helpmann's John looked, as Eric Keown said, like an emaciated Knave of Diamonds ; and, for me, Scofield's King Philip[1] was lost beneath the haggard, dyspeptic mask, the loam and rough-cast of the King of France, though I have to put it on record that it was this that caused one observer (Margaret Lane) to recall " the very face and figure of an Angevin stone king". Ivor Brown, too, found the Philip to be " richly alive in its testy, timorous way". I might have been happier if that other Philip, the Bastard, had not carried the day so memorably years before.

Hamlet was to come, and on the Birthday night, the last occasion but one on which there was a special Birthday première : a piece of local tradition it has appeared foolish to cast aside. (There has not been a Birthday Play since *A Midsummer Night's Dream* in 1949.) That afternoon in 1948, when the national flags billowed in colour from their triple rank of poles down the long slope of Bridge Street,

---

[1] King Philip has some of Shakespeare's most atrocious lines : a meditation on the tear that falls upon the hair of grief-wrought Constance :
Even to that drop ten thousand wiry friends
Do glue themselves in sociable grief,
Like true, inseparable, faithful loves,
Sticking together in calamity.

I felt it would have been a good idea to have entrusted the unfurling of the Danish flag to Scofield. I had noticed him earlier in the afternoon, leaning over the parapet of the Tramway Bridge and looking longingly towards the depths of Avon. The production at night proved to be an 1848 *Hamlet* in a romanticised Victorian-Gothic Elsinore, a Winterhalter-Waterhouse Doubting Castle of fretted arcades. Michael Benthall, the director, used a piece of special pleading. Hamlet was Everyman ; his problems were Everyman's in any age, and so forth. It seemed needless to talk of " vital contemporary relevance " : better, one felt, to suggest that it might be fun to see how *Hamlet* looked in frock-coat and crinoline.

As usual, one forgot the costumes not long after the play had begun. The most exciting phrase in the drama of the world is the simple " Who's there ? " spoken by Bernardo upon the platform before the castle. It is a question that we ask urgently of a new Hamlet himself. Can he say, in effect, " This is I, Hamlet the Dane", or have we to cry, with Laertes, " The Devil take thy soul ! "? Every watcher and listener has a private, an intimate Hamlet. I have long known the kind of man I want him to be. The character has been overlaid by words, by pedantic wrangling. Too many exegetists have been super-subtle about the play : more oddities have been written of it than of anything in the canon. (Who was it that, laughing at the dons, called Hamlet an Irishman ? He swears by St. Patrick, and he has a speechless Irish companion : " Now might I do it, Pat, now he is praying".) We should not blur the matter. Hamlet, appalled by his father's death, his mother's too hasty marriage, the Ghost's injunction, goes with horror to his task. While riven by doubt and fear—for has the Ghost deceived him but to damn him ?—other things add to his bitterness, his despair, his loathing of the " unweeded garden". There is the comfort of friendship with Horatio, " a man that fortune's buffets and rewards hast ta'en with equal thanks". For the rest

> The time is out of joint. O cursèd spite,
> That ever I was born to set it right !

He appears to be younger than we are told he is : young to be burdened with so terrible a duty. At core he is a sensitive boy longing for affection : his father dead, his mother disloyal, Ophelia lost—" Forty thousand brothers could not, with all their quantity of love, make up my sum." Prompted to his revenge by heaven and hell, he finds himself now, like Lear, bound upon a wheel of fire.

At Stratford Paul Scofield was a romantic, haunted Hamlet, "most dreadfully attended" by the thronging phantoms of his brain. Harold Hobson said he had "never seen a Hamlet more shot with the pale agony of irresolution". Elsewhere in the company I remember some of the trappings and the suits of woe : mutton-chop whiskers, for example, and the silk hat clapped on by Anthony Quayle's Claudius in the Churchyard as he uttered "Come, good Laertes " in those fuddled-bluffed tones of his. But I have forgotten Scofield's dress, his strapped trousers, the frock-coat. In memory now he is simply the timeless Hamlet. We heard Horatio's valediction not as a rubbed tag but as the farewell to a noble heart. Hamlet was a spirit in torment no less than his father. He would grow in eloquent detail and in variety of expression, but already he was in the royal presence. He saw his Hamlet—never a sentimentalised abstraction—by leaping torchlight, whereas Helpmann (in a reasoned, curiously cold study) might have been working in the glow of an electric candle. None could forget Scofield's pathos, the wrung heartbreak, face folded in grief, at " When you are desirous to be blessed, I'll blessing beg of you". We have known too many correct, almost formal Hamlets, aloof from Elsinore. Scofield was ever a prisoner within its bounds : the world held many confines, wards, and dungeons, Denmark being one of the worst. If an actor does not allow us to feel with him, to " purse up the heart", as John Garrett said Scofield did, no kind of mellifluous recitation, no external shows, will help.

A. V. Cookman, in a fine notice, spoke of this frail Hamlet as "a spiritual fugitive who seeks not so desperately the fulfilment of his earthly mission as some steadfast refuge for the hard-driven imagination. Only in death the refuge is found. It is the distinction of Mr. Scofield's playing that makes us free of this imagination, and its inner distractions have for us such intense dramatic reality that the melodramatic bustle of the court appears unreal, like the shadows outside Plato's cavern." Siriol Hugh Jones, in a similarly probing notice, called the Hamlet complex but not complicated. She observed how the great ratiocinative speeches sprang naturally from emotion, and she remarked, as critics have done so often, on Scofield's " almost motionless nervous excitement, peculiar to himself". Philip Hope-Wallace noted his " lenitive cadence and curious moth-like fragility". W. A. Darlington, in a despatch to the *New York Times*, said that what he really looked forward to was the Hamlet that Scofield would give in five years' time. There were complaints about too rapid diction, an arguable matter for much must depend on the listener's ear. And there was one review, appreciative but desperately pompous, from undergraduate Oxford, that in praising Scofield called him " a wandering plant, in sapless perambulation ".

That was the centre of the Stratford season and the first snow-peak of Paul Scofield's career. There was much else in 1948. He took over Bassanio in what T. C. Kemp called Michael Benthall's " choreographic canter " through Venice and Belmont. As Scofield played him, the young Venetian was never merely handsome pasteboard, yet remained a rather distant romantic : it was as if he did not really believe in the business of the caskets. One felt that his mind could be remote from Portia and her sunny locks, and pondering upon the idiocy of the dead Lord of Belmont :

> Ink clogs each casket : the whole piece is planned
> As a portentous exercise . . .

Roderigo, in Godfrey Tearle's production of *Othello,* was an unforgettable, a blistering sketch. It stings the mind even now. I do not imagine that Scofield's Roderigo had read Stanislavsky or that he had discovered what happened to him before the play began,[1] but it was obvious that he had his own bitter notion of the fellow, a peevish Venetian gull, flapping and wailing about the Cypriot shore. After the first act of *The Winter's Tale* had been battered to death by sheer noise (the cast, like the Dickensian family, was " composed of all the stateliest people thereabouts, and the noisiest "), Scofield came—as he did at Birmingham—straight from the wattle-cotes of Arden to the Bohemian pastoral : a slow, moony, furry-vowelled boy, going to buy sugar and currants

[1] Stanislavsky devotes a long passage to Roderigo's part (see *Stanislavsky Produces Othello*, pp. 14/16. Roderigo was " a simple fellow and always engaged in debauch". Once he "waylaid Desdemona in a dark canal, caught up with her gondola, and threw a huge bunch of flowers and a madrigal of his own composition into the craft," and so on.

and rice and saffron for the revel, or listening, a frozen shudder, great eyes staring, hair wild, to those torments thought up by the relishing Autolycus. We do not wonder that Dame Laura Knight painted a water-colour portrait of the Clown as she watched him from the wings of the Memorial Theatre. Sir Barry Jackson chose this painting as the official gift made to him at the end of his Stratford management.

Scofield's other part, in 1948, was Troilus. The play, venture in the satirical-heroic-didactic, is at times like a parching, gritty wind that raises the dust upon the plains of Troy. But it can heel the high lavolt. It achieves such loveliness as the words of Troilus :

> Her bed is India ; there she lies, a pearl ;
> Between our Ilium, and where she resides,
> Let it be called the wild and wandering flood . . .

or else forms the speeches of Ulysses like ice-patterns fronded upon a winter glass. At Stratford the play reached tragedy when Scofield's Troilus, already stricken, mourned at the last for Hector, his charged, low tones rough-edged as they struggled from a hell of grief and anger :

> Let him that will a screech-owl aye be call'd,
> Go into Troy and say there, " Hector's dead".

We left the theatre with this in our minds instead of the wry epilogue of Pandarus (" Your eyes, half out, weep out at Pandar's fall ") transferred to an earlier scene. Scofield, though it was not a part he reached easily, knew the rapture and the woe of Troilus. A. V. Cookman thought him miscast until he had taken Cressida's measure. It was a night of uncertainty ; but the production, generally frigid, blazed for a moment when Ulysses pointed to " yond towers, whose wanton tops do buss the clouds". We felt the rightful glory of the epic as Greeks and Trojans looked out towards us, and we saw tall Troy in their eyes.

VII

IT was good-bye at last to the Stratford Festival, but not to Stratford-upon-Avon. Terence Rattigan, much derided for it, had made an excursion into ancient history. On a night during the spring of

Angus McBean

1947 Memorial Theatre, Stratford-upon-Avon : Pericles in *Pericles, Prince of Tyre*

Angus McBean

1947 Lyric Theatre, Hammersmith : Young Fashion in *The Relapse,* with Richard Wordsworth (Coupler)

Angus McBean

1948   Memorial Theatre, Stratford-upon-Avon : King of France in *King John*,
with Ena Burrill (Constance)

Angus McBean

1948   Memorial Theatre, Stratford-upon-Avon : As Hamlet

Angus McBean

1948　Memorial Theatre, Stratford-upon-Avon : As Hamlet

Angus McBean

1948 Memorial Theatre, Stratford-upon-Avon : Bassanio in *The Merchant of Venice*, with Diana Wynyard (Portia)

Angus McBean

1948 Memorial Theatre, Stratford-upon-Avon : The Clown in *The Winter's Tale*, with John Kidd (Old Shepherd)

Angus McBean

1948   Memorial Theatre, Stratford-upon-Avon : Troilus in *Troilus and Cressida*, with Heather Stannard (Cressida)

Angus McBean

1948 Memorial Theatre, Stratford-upon-Avon: Roderigo in *Othello,* with
Anthony Quayle (Iago)

1949 Paul Scofield appeared again on the stage most familiar to
him.   The play was *Adventure Story*, on its provincial tour, and his
part was no less than Alexander the Great.   Scofield's only previous
acquaintance with Alexander (man who set out to conquer the world
before he had conquered himself) had been in *Love's Labour's Lost*.
Nathaniel, the curate—watched by Scofield's Armado as another
of the Worthies— was " a little o'erparted " :

> When in the world I liv'd, I was the world's
>   commander ;
> By east, west, north, and south, I spread my
>   conquering might.

Now Rattigan, already labelled and docketed, was condemned for
getting out of his snug pigeon-hole, for daring to toy with the
world's commander.   A fashionable dramatist had no right to be
covering these battles.   Critics said to him accusingly, in Armado's
words to the mocking Court on that other Worthy, Hector, " The
sweet war-man is dead and rotten . . . beat not the bones of the
buried."   In *Adventure Story* Alexander lay on his death-bed in
Babylon, wondering where his career had gone wrong.   At
journey's end we returned to the death-bed and to his amplified
musings.   Between prologue and epilogue the army from Macedon
drove across the eastern world, Issus, Gaugemela, Parthia, Bactria;
and slowly Alexander found himself corrupted by the temptations of
despotism : power without glory.   In spite of some Freudian
intrusions, it was a bold and largely successful simplification for the
theatre : Rattigan's own adventure story, but one unfortunate
enough to please neither the prickly-patronising (who shuddered
at the thought of a commercial dramatist o'erparted) nor the Aunt
Ednas in whom Rattigan has personified the comfortable middlebrow.

   Still, the play nearly came through.   Scofield could carry off
his first starring part in London, with its 6,000 words.   Richard
Findlater felt that, although the voice had strange vagaries of pitch
and tone, " drawling, precise, plummy, resonant", Scofield
simulated the pomp, charm, and hysteria of Alexander with regal
brilliance.   " One saw the Prince of Denmark at large in Asia
Minor."   Harold Hobson said : " All this fine actor's performances
have something of the other world about them.   Invariably he

looks as if he had been reading *The Turn of the Screw* and seen ghosts at midnight. His sonatas have spooks in them."

Joy Parker (who had been in Priestley's *Home Is To-morrow* during the previous autumn) rejoined her husband in *Adventure Story*. She did not speak, but her expressively shy barbarian chief's daughter Roxana—" a sort of princess in her own right " —was worth the journey from Macedon. She and her husband acted beautifully together in the scene where she chose the ring : " Yes, I think you'll make a good wife, Roxana. You also, I see, have the quality of luck." Soon after *Adventure Story* ended—it had a reasonable run for any dramatist but Rattigan—Scofield acted another conqueror, Tamburlaine the Great, in a radio version of Marlowe's play. There indeed the trumpets spoke. Scofield, who has one of the best radio voices, with a quality that sends the mind voyaging, made us see that Rattigan's play would have been helped by the Marlovian bounty of "great and thundering speech".

He went on from the despots to Constantin in Irene Hentschel's production of *The Seagull*, first at Hammersmith and again at the St. James's : a part in which many critics did not like him. He was accused of stiffness, even of a want of pathos, and various other crimes in the Tchehovian calendar. I found him extremely touching because he never o'erstepped the modesty of nature : this Hamlet had not forgotten the advice to the players. Throughout, Constantin felt, thought, communicated. Scofield—it cannot be said too often—is leagues from the mock-sensitive actor with tremolo in the voice and St. Vitus in the limbs, expressing emotion like a quivering crane-fly. Great grief is still : in the last numbed decision at Hammersmith Constantin's eyes told all.

During the run of *The Seagull* he managed, for a single night, to return to *Romeo and Juliet*. Romeo now ; he had the felicity of wooing Peggy Ashcroft's Juliet in the Balcony scene during a Sunday charity performance, a Coliseum night visited by troops of stars. Little remained to him except the Nurse, and no doubt that would arrive in time : he need not be impatient, and there was much at the moment to occupy him. Presently he moved forward to the play of cobweb-filigree that was to fix him firmly in London : *Ring Round the Moon*, Christopher Fry's version of *L'Invitation au Château*. It was the height of the Anouilh fashion. Scofield was cast for the double part of the twins who are forever chasing themselves, one a heartless schemer, one ingenuous and shy. Peter Brook, back with Scofield after three years, produced : I would have liked to have seen Brook and Christopher Fry as they discussed the production in the December austerity of the Lizard at the far south of Cornwall, waves high in Housel and the blade of the Lizard Light sweeping cliff and driven sea.

Brook, since Scofield had last acted with him, had been startling Covent Garden orthodoxy. Now he produced the Anouilh with a quick zest. It was moonshine with a Firbankian quality ; to describe it is to grasp a handful of moonlight. Among its personages, penned within a soaring Messel winter garden in spring, were Twins (one gentle, one bitter, both Scofield), a Crumbling Butler, a Secretive Secretary, a Faded Companion, a Melancholy Millionaire, a Lepidopterist, a Ballet Dancer, a Teacher of the Pianoforte, a General, and an Aunt (Margaret Rutherford, trumpeting like an imperious dragon-fly from her wheel-chair). In this fantastic diaphanous charade Scofield moved in a few seconds from heartlessness to diffidence, using the vibrant voice that—it was said with affection—could break, squeal, flatten out, startle by its unexpectedness, and yet delight. It was an extraordinarily elegant performance, much admired by the author : a compliment indeed from one who had watched Michel Bouquet's creation in Paris. Harold Hobson noted particularly, and shrewdly, the third act scene in which the young dancer Isabelle upbraided Hugo, as she thought, not realising that it was the twin Frédéric. During the whole of the long speech Scofield " stood absolutely motionless. His head was half-bowed, and his left arm hung at his side, the fingers loose and parted. They did not move by a fraction of an inch, until at the end of Isabelle's tirade Mr. Scofield raised his head, and one saw from the sad, concerned look on his face that he was not Hugo but Frédéric. . . . There was something extremely touching in the still and mute acceptance of undeserved reproach." It was, in fact, perfect Scofield. Throughout the years he had kept his natural qualities and sharpened his technique. Few players could indicate so much with so little fuss.

While he still made rings round the moon, while the tango was being danced, while Miss Rutherford was trumpeting, and Cecil Trouncer (millionaire with a carved-out Grinling Gibbons voice) shredded the banknotes, Scofield had two Sunday nights in *Pericles,*

Prince of Tyre, produced by his friend and former Stratford colleague, John Harrison, at the Rudolf Steiner Hall. They had long had faith in the Levantine adventure, even in its first act which Monck had cut so ruthlessly at Stratford. At this severely functional hall in the back-lands beyond Sherlock Holmes's end of Baker Street, *Pericles* was played uncut—moreover, without an interval. We passed right on from Gower's first speech to the reunion in the temple of Diana at Ephesus, and very few complained on a summer night like hot charcoal. Scofield could at last develop the entire character. The Shipboard and Recognition scenes were subtly voiced, and Pericles assumed his grieving age with more authority than at Stratford. Daphne Slater, again in the cast, now doubled Thaisa the mother and Marina the daughter: a warrantable partnership, most sensitively managed.

VIII

ANOUILH'S charade had to end, though it took its time about it : some two years. Scofield returned to Shakespeare. At the Phoenix (January, 1952) he joined John Gielgud in the comedy of *Much Ado About Nothing,* acted in the Mariano Andreu sets, an elaborate garden with niched gold statues, and a street, house, and church that folded and unfolded before our eyes. It was something at once simple and complex that might have puzzled Irving's designer, Telbin. London came to regard the production—one Stratford knew by heart—as the definitive revival of our day. *Much Ado* was written, as its Beatrice was born, under a dancing star ; but it cannot be merely romped through ; in Gielgud we had the right actor and director for the silken rhythms. He had Diana Wynyard as his Beatrice and Lewis Casson as Leonato. Scofield, persuasive and poised, gave his own touch of fantasy (one suspected that Mercutio was not far off) to Don Pedro of Arragon : "Your grace is too costly to wear every day", said Beatrice. It is a part that any actor of presence can sleek along competently. Paul Scofield has never looked upon acting as a confidence trick, and in *Much Ado* he created a personage. When, urbanely, Pedro left the Phoenix stage, he was still walking in

Leonato's garden or in the streets of Messina. No sign here of the once distinguished Pedro who, on being asked at rehearsal the significance of "What need the bridge much broader than the flood?" replied: "Blessed if I know, guv'nor". From the Phoenix performance I think yet of three lines towards the end:

> The wolves have preyed; and, look, the gentle day,
> Before the wheels of Phoebus, round about
> Dapples the drowsy east with spots of grey.

Scofield's utterance, his caressing of "Dapples the drowsy east," filled the mind with the first flaking silver of daybreak.

By now, at the age of thirty, Scofield had been for three years a star in his own right. He moved forward in the theatre with that strangely uncertain certainty of his, long-striding, delicate, noiseless: a growing lion-cub on hot bricks, said someone. After *Much Ado* he passed to a play by Charles Morgan, *The River Line*. He was an American, brusque, tortured, searching uncompromisingly for truth, resolved not to shirk responsibility, not to forget that, as a prisoner escaping in Occupied France, he had caused the death of a friend. The man had been suspected (without reason) of spying for the Germans: in such a predicament as this there was no time for nice inquiry. Here Mr. Morgan sought to mingle urgent drama with theatrically less urgent metaphysics. When his people were up-and-doing they held us; when they raked their souls, attention drifted. We were apt to fall into what Peacock's Mr. Flosky called the vulgar error of a man to whom "an unusual collocation of words, involving a juxtaposition of antiperistatical ideas, immediately suggested the notion of hyperoxysophistical paradoxology". Two Morgans might have had a hand in *The River Line*, its acts differed so sharply in texture. Pamela Brown, as a French girl in charge of a " station " on the escape line, developed a blow-lamp force. Scofield, strained and intense, animated a part that might have been wooden. Like his colleagues he was happiest in the second act; I can see him as he stared at his cards during that poker game in the granary at Toulouse, just before zero hour and Morgan's theatrical coup. The play went on first at the Edinburgh Festival. All work appears somehow to be better when you come to it from the presence of the Castle Rock, that shout in the sky, and leave it to drive out by a long road, another river line, beside the nighted Forth.

Morgan's drama travelled on from Edinburgh to the Lyric, Hammersmith, and later to the Strand Theatre. Scofield left the cast before Christmas 1952 (Phil Brown succeeded him) for the most important part he had yet had in London, Richard in *King Richard the Second* : one of three in a repertory season at the Lyric, Hammersmith. John Gielgud's name is now among the famous ones emblazoned on panels round the front of the circle and upon the ceiling. Scofield's should be there as well. At Hammersmith, in its last hours, this winter of 1952 added to its few distinctions : the setting sun and music at the close. We knew it to be an occasion from earliest curtain-rise upon the King, framed, so it looked, in gold, his favourites about him. The young Richard, with his heavy-lidded eyes and a cut-glass enunciation in which the words never jostled, but were defined and separated, could for a moment have been speaking in trance, guided by puppeteers behind his throne. Very soon he had established himself as true Richard, prey to the caterpillars of the commonwealth but ever conscious that he ruled by divine right. When this Richard's favourites were gone, it was as if a mask had been peeled from him. A gold symbol, spectre, eidolon of kingship turned to grief-riven humanity. At the renunciation, Richard was less of a " butterfly artist " (in the late Herbert Farjeon's phrase) with a poet's fancies, than a man who sought to gain time, to play with words, to keep for a moment longer the crown he must inevitably give. We heard throughout, and poignantly, the apprehension of doom, the note of "unking'd Richard". I had not known truer pathos in the couplet :

> Ay, no ; no, ay ; for I must nothing be ;
> Therefore no, no ; for I resign to thee.

We marked, too, how at the command, " Go, some of you convey him to the Tower", there was a pause before Richard, numbed, felt the humiliation of " convey " and pounced upon it in the high scorn of "O, good ! convey ? conveyors are you all . . ." As he lingered upon the stair, he heard Bolingbroke's " On Wednesday next we solemnly set down our coronation . . . " With a half-sob this "unking'd Richard " faltered from sight.

Scofield, never the " poetical play-actor", conscious artist in grief, failed in pathos only, and inexplicably, in the farewell to his Queen (Joy Parker, sorrow personified).[1] He was received with respect, though his voice still puzzled the critics—T. C. Worsley said that it moved between an angry rasp and die-away understatement—and Ivor Brown found the Richard, for all its scrupulous regard for character, to be curiously remote. John Gielgud, knowing every chopped comma in the text, had directed with generosity, but the décor went amiss. " Fair King Richard's land", as seen by Loudon Sainthill, was Toytown in effect, bandbox-fresh : we judged from these wispy sets that Richard played at being king of the castle : not a persuasive view of the grim tournament of the Middle Ages.

Congreve next, and fittingly in the theatre that had restored *The Way of the World* when Edith Evans's Millamant took the town. The revival was less fortunate. Gielgud, himself the producer, made music of Mirabell's protestations ; but he had in Pamela Brown a Millamant who thought too much : she was too studied for the dazzling languisher, and the exquisite raillery had a hard edge. Paul Scofield found no sort of difficulty with Witwoud (" I confess I do blaze to-day, I am too bright "), whinnying fop shrill with admiration at his own wit. But the revival will probably be remembered only as a hyphen between *Richard* and the resurrection of Otway's *Venice Preserv'd*, the last major English tragedy, an actor's rather than a poet's play that Gielgud had the wisdom to call from long neglect, in a production by Peter Brook. " Gentle Otway " is not very much read now, and his last appearance in London had been, astonishingly, as the author of *The Soldier's Fortune*. If he had watched the Lyric audience he would have deemed the silence, the expectancy, to be laurels to his stagecraft. Once they called him " next to Shakespeare " : not, I would say, for his language which runs directly and never floods into an Elizabethan cataract. It was a tribute, rather, to his play's dagger-keen thrust (it is a play of daggers), though I think the writing is better than J. W. Lambert believes.[2] Otway does humanise his

[1] Since *Adventure Story* she had appeared in such parts as Rosario in *The Romantic Young Lady* (Arts, 1949), Mashenka in *The Diary of a Scoundrel* (Arts, 1949), Belinda in *The Provok'd Wife* (Arts, 1950), Prudence in *The Hat Trick* (Duke of York's, 1950), Lady Precious Stream in Hsiung's play (Arts, 1950).

[2] " We . . . were surprised by the sheer theatrical force which fine acting could draw from a passable play written in barely passable verse."—Essay on *The Verse Drama* in the symposium, *Theatre Programme* (1954).

PAUL SCOFIELD

Jaffeir and Pierre, one impulsive, honourable, but too easily
overwrought (a fallen Brutus), his friend nobly undeviating in the
fight for liberty and ready at the last to encounter darkness like a
bride. It would have perplexed our ancestors to hear that *Venice
Preserv'd : A Plot Discover'd* could ever have been in the discard, a
play run to dust. *The Merchant of Venice, Othello, Venice Preserv'd :*
all must know these. Byron joined their names when he wrote in
the fourth canto of *Childe Harold :*

> Ours is a trophy which will not decay
> With the Rialto ; Shylock and the Moor,
> And Pierre, cannot be swept or worn away—
> The keystones of the arch !

Peter Brook did not try to force the tragedy or to fuss it, to
pamper it, as a fragile antique. Letting it declare itself untram-
melled, he honoured its past ; in the fourth act Dagger scene for
Jaffeir and Belvidera, he reminded us of Garrick and Mrs. Cibber
painted by Zoffany. I can recreate scene after scene as in a picture-
gallery : the chiaroscuro of the conspirators' heavy-arched cellar ;
the Senate enthroned against the darkly-glowing depths, the distances
of Leslie Hurry's set ; a to-and-fro by the lagoon's sombre calm, the
Execution scene suggested without dolorous parade. Byronic lines
I remembered were of Venice not as revel of the earth and masque
of Italy, but as the place where :

> though all were o'er,
> For us re-peopled were the solitary shore.

Philip Hope-Wallace called the play " rather noble and romantic
and morbid, like the paintings of Salvator Rosa". Paul Scofield in
smoulder and fire as Pierre, forthright, single-minded, might have
won applause from audiences that cheered the original actor,
William Scott of Betterton's company : a man who, on his record
elsewhere, should have offered " a polished elegance of manner,
with just the right freedom and cavalier bravado, but no swagger or
bluster". John Gielgud made passionately genuine the love-and-
friendship conflict in Jaffeir. A superb partnership. Scofield
(" Cursed be your Senate ! Cursed your constitution ! ") had
never been more intense. The word has had its power reduced by

68

Angus McBean

1949 St. James's Theatre : Alexander in *Adventure Story*, with Joy Parker
(Roxana)

Angus McBean

1949 St. James's Theatre : Alexander in *Adventure Story*, with Julian Dallas
(Hephaestion) and Gwen Ffrangcon-Davies (Queen Mother of Persia)

Angus McBean

1949   Lyric Theatre, Hammersmith : Constantin in *The Seagull*

Houston Rogers

1950   Globe Theatre : Frédéric in *Ring Round the Moon*

Houston Roger

1950　Globe Theatre : Hugo in *Ring Round the Moon*

application to three-minute fragments, minor speeches. But one can use it with full value for *Venice Preserv'd*. Certainly the symbol of the play might be a dagger. It was with his dagger that Jaffeir, who answered the call of Belvidera to betray friend and faction, redeemed his treachery by a double stroke. An attendant Officer has the only word possible : '' Heaven grant I die so well ! ''

IX

PAUL SCOFIELD, at the end of 1953, came back to modern dress in Wynyard Browne's *A Question of Fact*. It was done at the Piccadilly Theatre which really needs a rousting musical piece ; a serious play can be frozen unless you are seated well up in the stalls. *A Question of Fact* survived, and it would have been a crime if it had not : its author is one of the most honest dramatists and sure craftsmen now working for our stage. The play, potent and veracious, is in effect a study of various aspects, various levels, of imagination : '' So many shapes hath Fancy ! '' Scofield appeared as a young public schoolmaster newly married. An adopted child, with no idea of his parentage, he learns now that his father had been a murderer. The past closes in. Though the mist is opaque, his too anxious imagination pierces it. What kind of man was this unknown father ? How did he come to murder ? How easy is a bush supposed a bear ! At length the mother, her entry cunningly delayed, resolves the problem : it is one to send the audience away arguing. At the Piccadilly Scofield himself was splendidly right. Few can look backwards as he does ; each crack in his questing voice seemed to be another loophole upon the past. It was frightening to watch the man, perplexed in the extreme, as he sought reassurance, allowed his fancy to seek forbidden paths. There were moments of taut emotion that reminded me, without irrelevance, of the lines from a Sussex poem, '' See you our stilly woods of oak, and the dread ditch beside''. Scofield is an actor as English as his Sussex home (he lives now at Balcombe) ; in *A Question of Fact* he was hardly recognisable as the brooding young American of *The River Line*. One would have said of the company (Gladys Cooper and Pamela Brown were in it) that the fleet of stars was anchored and the young star-captain glowed.

The play took him well into 1954. At the end of the year he was back in London with Anouilh. Inherently English though he is, he has established his own *entente cordiale*. At the Lyric, Hammersmith—now, so to speak, a stage as responsive to the hilts as Stratford had been—one of the early *pièces roses*, *Léocadia*, became, in its English text, *Time Remembered*. It was for me a loss. Thought dwelt on a man who had sensuously combined the feel of velvet with the taste of chocolate and the scent of violets. In that recipe there was also the note of a bugle, but *Time Remembered* had only the cloying ingredients. The piece, which might have as its epigraph, " Ere the parting hours go by, Quick, thy tablets, Memory ! " is an invention, a fantasy, about a young Prince in thrall to the memory of a dead ballerina. (She had strangled herself by accident, with a scarf, and not before it was time.) His aunt the Duchess— all Anouilh in a phrase—tries to cheer him by bringing to the Breton estate the properties, taxi-cab, night-club, ice-cream cart even, of the transient affair with Léocadia. For verisimilitude she hires a little milliner who is apparently Léocadia's image, and who must be trained to blink, to nibble orchids, and generally to behave as the original did in life. At Hammersmith Mary Ure made her name as this Amanda in Wonderland ; Margaret Rutherford wavered about like a balloon in the light evening airs (beneath her the slithy toves were gimbling) ; and Scofield acted the doleful Albert with his evocatively sombre-romantic command. None could have done it better ; but it was a soggy part (even if he had the tingling joy of entering upon a bicycle), and he must have looked back a shade sadly to his months in *A Question of Fact*. The play remained elusive—not even a ring round the moon—and decorative though its settings were, we had visualised something remoter and stranger for that Breton estate. We should have known that the wild woods of Broceliande were not far away. As it was, we felt this only in the cadence of Scofield's voice : he does not prettify a phrase but none can evoke more readily a twilit landscape or a mood achingly wistful.

Cinema men—and it was very natural—had been seeking him for years. He had turned down a Hollywood offer in November 1946 after his first Stratford Festival. Scofield held to the theatre :

it was not until 1955 that his first film was shown when he appeared (with Olivia de Havilland) as Philip of Spain in *That Lady*.   Darryl Zanuck, the production chief, said of him : " That actor ! The best I have seen since John Barrymore."   Philip was the sad, bigoted despot who sent the Armada against England, the vast fleet that (in a Cornish phrase) was all but " scat to flinders".   *That Lady*, from Kate O'Brien's novel, confined itself to matters domestic : Scofield put on Philip's years like a cloak, one that did not sag loosely about him as about so many young actors terrified of age.   Paul Dehn spoke of the intricate make-up " like eroded marble.   The eyes seem to need de-scaling, the voice itself is dusted over, and he walks with the gingerly foreboding of the acutely arthritic.   Yet he remains every twisted inch a king."   A creation, then : " one of the small gallery of classic screen portraits", said Campbell Dixon.   The British Film Academy chose Scofield as " the most promising newcomer to films " in 1955.   One wished that he could have had such a text as Masefield's in the short play of *Philip the King* :

> In bitter days
> The soul finds God, God us.

Perhaps Scofield may yet act this in the theatre or upon radio.

He has long been a governing sound-radio actor.   Towards the end of January 1955, he appeared as Edward the Second—Edward of Carnarvon, that is, who was the great-grandfather of Richard the Second and who, like him, died for the sweet fruition of an earthly crown.   Scofield's vocal virtuosity raised for us such lines as " This isle shall fleet upon the ocean And wander to the unfrequented Inde".   He hurtled at Edward's passionate outbreaks, and those Berkeley scenes branded the imagination : the murderer's " Foh ! " as he pushed back the door of the " lake", the dungeon-sewer where Edward lay ; the King's voice that would have forced tears from granite ; a shriek that chilled the night by Severn.   I remember other radio occasions : how Scofield reached the heart of the matter (without portentous attitudes) in a version of Obey's *Lazarus*, self-conscious extension of the eleventh chapter of St. John's Gospel ; and how, in *The Duchess of Malfi*, with Peggy Ashcroft, his lycanthropic Ferdinand flared at " I have this night digged up a mandrake", and continued to flare.   I do not often recall that, as a modern critic assures us, " in Webster, as in the best Continental drama, reality is conceived as psychological truth in its all-embracing Existential sense", but I do hear Scofield's voice—nearer, I think, to the dramatist. " We'll *hear* a play", said Hamlet : Scofield appreciates that.[1] He knows, too, Cibber on Betterton : " In the delivery of Poetical Numbers . . . it is scarce credible upon how minute an Article of Sound depends their greatest Beauty or Inaffection." A pebble can remain a pebble, or it can be powdered of a sudden with glinting mica.

x

WE'LL hear a play. So, at last, back to *Hamlet,* after seven years (W. A. Darlington had asked for five). Peter Brook produced, the first event of a Scofield-Brook season that would cover *Hamlet, The Power and the Glory* (based upon Graham Greene's novel), and Eliot's *The Family Reunion* at the Phoenix, and go thence to America. *Hamlet* began with an extraordinary prospect : Scofield would act in Moscow in the first English company to appear there since the 1917 revolution. A nice tour list : Brighton (two weeks), Oxford, Birmingham, Moscow. I went up to *Hamlet* during the fourth week of the tour. It was at Birmingham, in the Alexandra Theatre, just over ten years since that autumn matinee at the " Rep " : also a Brook production. Midland playgoers, massed on a drizzling night, had an experience for the records. In a chameleon-set by Georges Wakhevitch, an arched hall with its various windows, crannies, galleries put to inventive use, Brook produced with the directness of a master. Hamlet was not discovered, brooding and aloof in the room of state, the gloomy Dane of *cliché*. When the battlements had faded, and light blocked in for us the hall with its receding arches, there Hamlet stood, gazing round him sadly before going to his place : a frail, lithe figure in conventional black, the gold chain round his neck, his eyes dark

---

[1] He has also appeared on radio as Berowne in *Love's Labour's Lost,* as Tamburlaine, Alexander the Great (*Adventure Story*), Chopin, and Axël in Villiers de l'Isle Adam's play ; and in *The Cross and the Arrow, The Bronze Horse, The Nameless One of Europe,* Anouilh's *Eurydice* (*Point of Departure*), *Henry the Eighth* (Dame Sybil Thorndike's jubilee performance), and the serialised version of Henry James's *Portrait of a Lady.*

76

with sorrow, the sweet (but never sentimentalised) prince, observed of all observers, who must become a soul in travail : the troubled soul of Denmark living, still to be summoned by the soul of Denmark dead.

I have known many touching Hamlets. Only Scofield has gone at once to the heart. He did this at Stratford in the Victorian-Gothic frame. He did so in the less distracting décor of the Brook revival ; again emotion was not simply fabricated to fit the words. We took with him the progress through Hamlet's mind : a journey marked by such things as the cry of " Father ! " in hopeless longing ; the anguished " O cursèd spite ! " arms flung wide, all tragedy in that wind-blown, husky-shining voice ; the early tenderness for Ophelia (drawn closely to him as he spoke) ; the homage to Horatio, given with quiet urgency while sitting on the players' property skip ; a reversion (so it seemed to me) to an older manner, that of Macready's day, at the full drive of " 'Tis now the very witching time of night " ; the moment during the Closet scene when, boy again, his head drooped upon Gertrude's shoulder (" When you are desirous to be blest, I'll blessing beg of you ") ; the Churchyard philosophy and the Churchyard brag ; the acceptance before the duel, Hamlet rapt as he approached his resolution ; and last, the gentleness and royalty in the voice, very Hamlet, as in death he bequeathed name and story to the keeping of his friend. Many have taken us on Hamlet's progress, prompted to revenge by heaven and hell ; for me Scofield, with his rifted voice, one that can bring an image of light diffused and fretted across a broken classic column, has been essentially the man. Agreed, this or that shade of emotion has been expressed more precisely, that scene more firmly driven ; A. (or perhaps B.) could be less at odds with the phrasing (the " quintessence of dust " speech, for example) ; and certainly— the word here is Agate's, pre-Scofield—the floor of this Hamlet's mind does lack its rotting boards. Let be. Nowhere has the Hamlet that I know—and I can but speak for myself—risen from the text more poignantly.

At Birmingham he was, I felt, most affecting when he looked at the body of Polonius and said, his anger flickering to stillness, " I do repent ". The prelude to the duel, " If it be now, 'tis not to come", when all is on the hazard, may be Scofield's for history. There must always be debate over his rendering of the verse.

Blessedly, he is never a marmoreal reciter. Striving for the sense, in the great soliloquies he did not lose the sound. We heard in "How all occasions" how everything was expressed in a passage of desperate music that beat at brain and heart. The test of any Hamlet is what we remember of it in years ahead ; there will be time for reckoning and retrospect. Some critics, when Scofield reached the Phoenix Theatre in December 1955, found him too restrained. Anthony Hartley, for one, felt that "the dæmonic, brutal character of the Renaissance prince was much underplayed, and we are left with Renaissance melancholy, the muted note of a sonnet by Du Bellay or a lyric by Nashe". Others mourned for the younger Stratford Scofield. But any Hamlet must meet a house divided. "What man is there, now living", exclaimed that notable critic, Mrs. Curdle, "who can present before us all those changing and prismatic colours with which the character is invested ? " I cannot recall one more able to communicate suffering without emotional theatrics, pitch-and-toss. Nothing was externalised ; Scofield did not merely simulate a sorrow. We should be glad that this foredoomed Renaissance prince with the ravaged brow could lead our players to Moscow, and to Stanislavsky's stage.

Such artists as Diana Wynyard (Gertrude), Mary Ure (Ophelia), Ernest Thesiger (Polonius), and Alec Clunes (the King) helped him to people the Court of Denmark. The fortnight's visit to Russia— a " date " wedged oddly between Birmingham and London— passed like fantasy : the flight (Claudius and Polonius in fur hats) ; airport lights in dazzle upon the Moscow snow ; an emotional welcome to warm the nipping and eager air ; the hotel and the Scofields' anachronistic suite, looking like a page from *Anna Karenina ;* playbills that announced what seemed to be " *Gamlet* " ; the hallowed Moscow Art Theatre, Stanislavsky's own, its seagull on the curtain ; cheers at the première, and nearly twenty curtain-calls ; audiences eagerly responsive, though just one beat behind the players. Much more : the exhilaration of the dry cold, many degrees under zero ; Russian surprise at finding even the three-and-a-half hours' *Hamlet* so short (in Moscow they run to length) ; daily skirmishing in the street, for the play had been televised and all Moscow demanded a word and an autograph ; the sight of Stalin lying embalmed ; the constant shock of Muscovite architecture,

Houston Rogers

1952   Phoenix Theatre : Don Pedro in *Much Ado About Nothing*

Angus McBean

1952 Lyric Theatre, Hammersmith : Philip Sturgess in *The River Line*

Angus McBean

1952   Lyric Theatre, Hammersmith : Richard in *King Richard II*, with Eric
Porter (Bolingbroke)

1953   Lyric Theatre, Hammersmith : Witwoud in *The Way of the World*

through the baroque to the most functional of flats ; receptions,[1] parties, pictures, caviare, vodka, Ministerial speeches ; hundreds of Russian players at the airport to see the company off ; and a moment when, on the final wing of the journey, in an aircraft from West Berlin, all forty of the British actors, snow on their boots, fell asleep as on a rehearsed cue. It was tiring and exciting. The company felt that the Iron Curtain, as well as the Art Theatre curtain, had been lifted for it. Peter Brook called the Moscow seagull a symbol of the tour : " We never touched ground". The visitors found themselves in a playgoing city, among people bred to the classic theatre and to the ballet, used to the best and cherishing tradition, as in the run of a renowned and unstoppable production of *The Three Sisters*. Russian actors were astonished that a major play could be presented a dozen times within ten days ; there twice or thrice a month was the rule for strenuous parts. Besides praising the dramatic and intellectual merits of Scofield's Hamlet, Moscow critics had generous admiration for an endurance test.

Every first night is an ordeal, and that of a Hamlet especially. At the London première (the Phoenix) of what will live in stage shorthand as " the Moscow *Hamlet*", Paul Scofield must have felt seasoned. Certainly he would hardly find again anything sterner than the televising in Moscow of the Nunnery scene. For this a leading Russian actor and actress, then in *Hamlet* at a provincial theatre farther from Moscow than Moscow from London, were flown back to the capital. The Russian Hamlet played the scene with the English Ophelia, Mary Ure ; and Scofield undertook the scene with the Russian actress. He spoke in English at his own tempo, she in Russian at hers. Heavily equipped with business (a long scarf appeared to be important), she wept as naturally and freely during the bi-lingual duet as she was accustomed to do in her own production. It went off well, though it sounds to us like a private war of the roses : the Russian " rose of May " and the English " expectancy and rose of the fair state".

Joy Parker[2] went to Moscow with her husband. In England they

---

[1] Exhausted and thirsty after a performance, Scofield attended one of the chain of official receptions and saw upon a side-table a large china jug, like a piece of old-fashioned washstand-ware, filled with a colourless liquid. Obviously water. Relieved, he poured out a glassful and drank deep. It was excellent vodka, and his conversation that night had rarely been more spirited.

[2] She has appeared since 1953 in such plays as *The Fifth Season* and two productions of *The Marvellous History of Puss-in-Boots*.

are faithful to Sussex, living at Balcombe with their son Martin and their daughter Sarah who was born in 1951. The private and the stage lives of the Scofields do not mingle. There is no question here of gossip-column fodder, and it can never be said of them that they give a better performance off the stage than on it.

XI

PAUL SCOFIELD, who was not yet thirty-four, received the C.B.E. in the New Year Honours list of 1956. His *Hamlet* would have the third longest unbroken run in English stage history.[1] It was not much more than twenty years since the school plays at Varndean—the Juliet and the Rosalind—and only ten since critics made, as it were, a formal discovery of Scofield in the blossomed Stratford April of 1946. The notices of the Festival merely ratified what Birmingham had said already. With Scofield has marched Peter Brook. The Repertory *King John* ; the Stratford *Love's Labour's Lost* and *Romeo and Juliet* : the West End *Ring Round the Moon*; then *Venice Preserv'd*, the Moscow *Hamlet*, the Phoenix Theatre season: it has been an uncommon partnership of artist and director.

Hamlet, at the Phoenix, gave way in April, 1956, to a version of Graham Greene's *The Power and the Glory*. Scofield startled many playgoers still unprepared for his command as a character actor. Those who knew him at Birmingham and Stratford were less astonished. He played a shrivelled, wizened, " whisky priest " on the run, the last priest left in the corruption, the squalor, and the brutality of a Mexican state misgoverned by a ruthless anti-clerical junta. Shrunken, almost unrecognisable, his gait a shamble, his voice parched, Scofield created the man as excitingly as Brook created the environment. Far from a saint on earth, the little man knows that, whatever he may have done, he has still the power of saving others. It is this that aids him in his last colloquy with the Lieutenant of Police. Cut down the tree of faith, and the world must wither.

[1] 124 performances.

Another voice is heard :
And now I know
That my business is not to run away,
                    but to pursue,
Not to avoid being found, but to seek.

It is the voice of T. S. Eliot's Harry, Lord Monchesney, in *The Family Reunion*, a play that has always worried people who are out of key with the dramatist. His admirers accept as an absorbing spiritual exercise this tale of sin and expiation, with its modern fabric on a base of classical myth. Others, finding the verse arid, share the author's own doubtful second thoughts. Even so, during June, 1956, both groups joined at the Phoenix to applaud Peter Brook's production (with its subtle suggestion of the Erinyes who become the Eumenides), and the acting of Dame Sybil Thorndike, eloquent in watchful silence as in speech, Gwen Ffrangcon-Davies as Agatha (" There are hours when there seems to be no past or future "), and Paul Scofield as the burdened wanderer who must go at last to " follow the bright angels ". For this part Scofield's tones became a sable silvered ; he looked into the man's soul and revealed to us what he saw. " Whether," A. V. Cookman wrote next morning, " as the sleepless-eyed youth flying with pale haunted face from the Furies, or as the suddenly spiritually-composed fugitive turning pursuer and flying towards the purgatorial flame, Mr. Scofield speaks as a man who feels every word."

Paul Scofield, as much as anyone now playing, has what we must call magnetism. Whenever he appears in the theatre he is a personage. The ranks divide : you cannot hide him among the ruck, and his acting has a stereoscopic quality. Yet he has never taken the centre of the stage as his right. Never was anyone less arrogant : he seems often to be gently surprised at his own eminence. Sometimes still he can pace the stage as on a tight-rope, or as one bridging " a current roaring loud On the unsteadfast footing of a spear", unsure whether he will reach the other side. (We know that he will ; his footing is as secure as Blondin's above Niagara.) His voice, too, can have a tentative, probing approach. It asks the way. The country is new about him : he wonders, as we do, what can open up round the corner. We never fear, as with less sensitive artists, that acting has become a matter of adjusting a gramophone needle, that a cigarette will be chosen and lit in twelve precisely-rehearsed movements. Scofield recreates a part nightly : that is why, towards the end of a long run, we never see him in a washed-out carbon copy of the first performance.

He has gifts that we recall in the late Ion Swinley : a similar virility, unexpected elegance (Hugo and Frédéric ; Don Pedro ; Albert), and a natural sense of period which means simply that he can wear the costume of a given period without waving a ticket for the Chelsea Arts Ball. He can remind us, too, of Swinley's haunted-man look, that unmatched wistfulness, unveiling of the past :

> For he is like to something I remember,
> A great while since, a long, long time ago.

But comparison must rest, for Paul Scofield is at once very much himself and rarely like himself. One thing is sure : he is a major classical actor. It would be unwise to thrust him into any pigeon-hole. A man who can play Hamlet and Cloten, Armado and Witwoud, Mercutio and the Clown (*la vie de Bohème*), Pierre, the Priest, and that sad poppet of the Aguecheeks, is not to be labelled dogmatically—unless, of course, we reach for the gum in repeating that he is " not always Scofield". I feel that he works most easily when the man has a fantastic strain or stands apart from his fellows. He is the last actor in Britain to be wasted on some standard off-the-peg hero, the routine trifler of West End commerce.

Scofield wants a character he can explore with an independent mind. His mannerisms are, theatrically, those of an explorer, a seeker of new paths. Whatever he may do in future, nothing will be just trivial, mildly competent. If his approach is tentative, we know that suddenly voice and imagination will flash together. Already he leads the younger actors. In the theatre, Paul Scofield, born not to sue but to command (and still quietly astonished), is without question heir-apparent to the throne.

Angus McBean

1953 Lyric Theatre, Hammersmith : Pierre in *Venice Preserv'd*, with David Dodimead (Duke of Venice), Herbert Lomas (Priuli) and Geoffrey Taylor (Officer)

Angus McBean

1953   Piccadilly Theatre : Paul Gardiner in *A Question of Fact*, with Pamela
Brown (Rachel Gardiner)

Angus McBean

1954 Lyric Theatre, Hammersmith : The Prince in *Time Remembered*, with Mary Ure (Amanda) and Margaret Rutherford (The Duchess of Pont-au-Bronc)

1955 Art Theatre, Moscow : As Hamlet

CAREER OF PAUL SCOFIELD

STAGE

1939   Student at Croydon Repertory Theatre School

1940   London Mask Theatre School (Principal: John Fernald) at Westminster Theatre

January   Walked on in *Desire Under The Elms* by Eugene O'Neill, Westminster Theatre (Dir. : Henry Cass)

April   Third Clerk and First Soldier in *Abraham Lincoln* by John Drinkwater, Westminster Theatre (Dir.: Henry Cass)

August   Walked on in *Cornelius* by J. B. Priestley, Westminster Theatre (Dir. : Henry Cass)

Autumn—

1941
Spring   At Bideford Repertory Theatre, N.Devon (directed by Eileen Thorndike and Herbert Scott) in such parts as:
King Lear, Macbeth, and Petruchio (*The Taming of the Shrew*) in programme of Shakespearean extracts
Dan in *Night Must Fall* by Emlyn Williams
Tom Pettigrew in *Berkeley Square* by John L. Balderston (in collaboration with J. C. Squire)
Albert Feather in *Ladies in Retirement* by Edward Percy and Reginald Denham
Prosper in *Granite* by Clemence Dane
Richard Greatham in *Hay Fever* by Noël Coward
George Pepper in *Red Peppers*, Alec Harvey in *Still Life*, and Henry Gow in *Fumed Oak*, in three one-act plays by Noël Coward, forming a *To-night at Eight-Thirty* programme.

Summer   With Eileen Thorndike and Herbert Scott's company at Houghton Hall, Cambridge as Noah in *Noah* by André Obey, translated by Arthur Wilmurt

Autumn   Vincentio, and later Tranio, in E.N.S.A. tour of *The Taming of the Shrew* by William Shakespeare (Dir. : Robert Atkins)

1942

Spring	Rehearses Messenger in the *Medea* of Euripides (Dir. : Lewis Casson) for C. E. M. A. tour in Wales ; mumps intervenes, and he does not appear
March	Hotel Clerk in tour of *Jeannie* by Aimée Stuart (Dir.: Noël Plant)
June	Ainger in tour of *Young Woodley* by John van Druten (Dir.: Kathleen O'Regan)
September	Stephen Undershaft in *Major Barbara* by Bernard Shaw, Repertory Theatre, Birmingham (Travelling Repertory Theatre ; Dir. : John Moody)

1942

October	Horatio in *Hamlet, Prince of Denmark* by William Shakespeare, Repertory Theatre, Birmingham (Travelling Repertory Theatre; Dir.: Basil C. Langton)

Winter to

1943

Spring	Major Sergius Saranoff in *Arms and the Man* by Bernard Shaw: C.E.M.A. tour of munition hostels (Travelling Repertory Theatre)
June	Alex Morden in *The Moon Is Down* by John Steinbeck, Whitehall Theatre (Dir.: Basil C. Langton)
Autumn	Donald in *Three-Cornered Moon* by Gertrude Tonkonogy: C.E.M.A. tour of munition hostels (Travelling Repertory Theatre: Dir.: Basil C. Langton)

December—

1944

January	At Theatre Royal, Bristol, in Travelling Repertory Theatre productions (Dir. : Basil C. Langton,) as : The Stranger in *The Cricket on the Hearth* adapted by Sir Barry Jackson from Charles Dickens's novel Donald in *Three-Cornered Moon* by Gertrude Tonkonogy Tybalt in *Romeo and Juliet* by William Shakespeare
Spring	Oliver Farrant in *I Have Been Here Before* by J. B. Priestley: C.E.M.A. tour of munition hostels.

Autumn—

1945

Summer	A member of the Birmingham Repertory Theatre Company, appearing as :

Prince Po and First Coolie in *The Circle of Chalk*, adapted by Klabund from the Chinese ; English version by James Laver (Dir. : John Moody)

Reginald Bridgnorth in *Getting Married* by Bernard Shaw (Dir. : John Moody)

The Clown in *The Winter's Tale* by William Shakespeare (Dir. : H. K. Ayliff)

William D'Albini in *The Empress Maud* by Andrew Leigh (Dir. : H. K. Ayliff)

Toad in *Toad of Toad Hall* by A. A. Milne from Kenneth Grahame's *The Wind in The Willows* (Dir. : John Moody)

Valentine in *Doctor's Delight* adapted by Sir Barry Jackson from Molière's *Le Malade Imaginaire* (Dir. : John Moody)

A Fisherman in *Land's End* by F. L. Lucas (Dir. : John Moody)

Young Marlow in *She Stoops To Conquer* by Oliver Goldsmith (Dir. : John Moody)

Constantin in *The Seagull* by Anton Tchekhov (Dir. : John Moody)

Jerry Devine in *Juno and the Paycock* by Sean O'Casey (Dir. : John Moody)

Autumn At the Birmingham Repertory Theatre as :

John Tanner in *Man and Superman* by Bernard Shaw (Dir. : Peter Brook)

Philip Faulconbridge (the Bastard) in *King John* by William Shakespeare (Dir. : Peter Brook)

Doctor Wangel in *The Lady From The Sea* by Henrik Ibsen (Dir. : Peter Brook)

St. Patrick, A Crusader, Colonel Bygadsby, etc., in *1066 And All That* adapted by Reginald Arkell

1946

20th April—
28th
September   A member of the Festival Company at the Shake-
speare Memorial Theatre, Stratford-upon-Avon, as:
Cloten in *Cymbeline* by William Shakespeare (Dir. :
Nugent Monck)

Don Adriano de Armado in *Love's Labour's Lost* by
William Shakespeare (Dir. : Peter Brook)

King Henry V in *King Henry the Fifth* by William
Shakespeare (Dir. : Dorothy Green)

Oliver in *As You Like It* by William Shakespeare
(Dir. : H. M. Prentice)

Malcolm in *Macbeth* by William Shakespeare (Dir. :
Michael MacOwan)

Lucio in *Measure for Measure* by William Shakespeare
(Dir.: Frank McMullan)

November   Tegeus-Chromis in *A Phoenix Too Frequent* by
Christopher Fry, Arts Theatre Club, London
(Dir. : Noel Willman)

1947

5th April—
27th
September   At the Shakespeare Memorial Theatre, Stratford-
upon-Avon as :
Mercutio in *Romeo and Juliet* by William Shakespeare
(Dir. : Peter Brook)

Mephistophilis in *The Tragical History of Doctor
Faustus* by Christopher Marlowe (Dir.: Walter Hudd)

Lucio in *Measure For Measure* by William Shakespeare
(Frank McMullan's production re-staged byRonald
Giffen)

Don Adriano de Armado in *Love's Labour's Lost*
by William Shakespeare (Dir. : Peter Brook)

Sir Andrew Aguecheek in *Twelfth Night* by William
Shakespeare (Dir. : Walter Hudd)

Pericles in *Pericles, Prince of Tyre* by William
Shakespeare (Dir. : Nugent Monck)

Angus McBean

1955   Phoenix Theatre : As Hamlet, with Michael David (Horatio), John Turner (Marcellus) and John Phillips (Ghost)

Armstrong Jones

1956 Phoenix Theatre : A Priest in *The Power and the Glory*

Armstrong Jones

1956 Phoenix Theatre : Harry, Lord Monchesney in *The Family Reunion,* with Sybil Thorndike (Amy, Dowager Lady Monchesney)

Twentieth Century Fox

1955 Film : Philip of Spain in *That Lady*

October	With the Stratford-upon-Avon company as Mercutio in *Romeo and Juliet* and Sir Andrew in *Twelfth Night* during a short London season at His Majesty's Theatre
December	Young Fashion in *The Relapse ; or, Virtue In Danger* by Sir John Vanbrugh, Lyric Theatre, Hammersmith. Transferred in January 1948 to the Phoenix Theatre (Dir.: Anthony Quayle)

1948

15th April—30th

October · At the Shakespeare Memorial Theatre, Stratford-upon-Avon, as :

Philip, King of France in *King John* by William Shakespeare (Dir. : Michael Benthall)

Bassanio in *The Merchant of Venice* by William Shakespeare (Dir. : Michael Benthall)

Hamlet in *Hamlet, Prince of Denmark* by William Shakespeare (Dir. : Michael Benthall)

The Clown in *The Winter's Tale* by William Shakespeare (Dir. : Anthony Quayle)

Troilus in *Troilus and Cressida* by William Shakespeare (Dir. : Anthony Quayle)

Roderigo in *Othello, the Moor of Venice* by William Shakespeare (Dir. : Godfrey Tearle)

1949

March	Alexander in *Adventure Story* by Terence Rattigan, St. James's Theatre (Dir.: Peter Glenville)
October	Treplef (Constantin Gavrilovitch) in *The Seagull* by Anton Tchehov, George Calderon's version, Lyric Theatre, Hammersmith. Transferred in November to the St. James's Theatre (Dir.: Irene Hentschel)
20th November	Romeo in the Balcony scene of *Romeo and Juliet* (Peggy Ashcroft as Juliet) in " . . . *Merely Players,*" London Coliseum

1950

January   Hugo, "a young man about town", and Frédéric, his twin brother, in *Ring Round the Moon,* a charade with music (*L'Invitation au Château*) by Jean Anouilh, translated by Christopher Fry, Globe Theatre (Dir.: Peter Brook).

July   Pericles in two Sunday night performances of *Pericles, Prince of Tyre* by William Shakespeare, Rudolf Steiner Hall (Under Thirty Theatre Group: Dir.: John Harrison)

6th

November   Appeared as Pryce Ridgeley in the second act of *His House In Order* by Sir Arthur Pinero, Irene Vanbrugh Memorial Performance, Theatre Royal, Drury Lane (matinee)

1952

January   Don Pedro, Prince of Arragon in *Much Ado About Nothing* by William Shakespeare, Phoenix Theatre (Dir. : John Gielgud)

August   Philip Sturgess in *The River Line* by Charles Morgan, Lyceum Theatre (Edinburgh), Edinburgh Festival. Thence to the Lyric Theatre, Hammersmith and, later, to the Strand Theatre (Dir.: Michael MacOwan)

December   Richard the Second in *King Richard the Second* by William Shakespeare, Lyric Theatre, Hammersmith (Dir.: John Gielgud)

1953

February   Witwoud in *The Way of the World* by William Congreve, Lyric Theatre, Hammersmith (Dir.: John Gielgud)

May   Pierre in *Venice Preserv'd* by Thomas Otway, Lyric Theatre, Hammersmith (Dir. : Peter Brook)

December   Paul Gardiner in *A Question of Fact* by Wynyard Browne, Piccadilly Theatre (Dir.: Frith Banbury)

1954

31st May   Charles Surface in Screen Scene from *The School For Scandal* by Richard Brinsley Sheridan, Sybil Thorndike Jubilee matinee, Her Majesty's Theatre.

December   Prince Albert Troubiscoi in *Time Remembered by* Jean Anouilh, English version by Patricia Moyes of *Léocadia*, Lyric Theatre, Hammersmith ; later transferred to New Theatre (Dir.: William Chappell)

1955

November   Hamlet in *Hamlet, Prince of Denmark*, Art Theatre, Moscow (Dir. : Peter Brook)

December   Hamlet at Phoenix Theatre, London

1956

April   A Priest in *The Power and the Glory*, adapted by Denis Cannan and Pierre Bost from Graham Greene's novel, Phoenix Theatre (Dir.: Peter Brook)

June   Harry, Lord Monchesney, in *The Family Reunion*, by T. S. Eliot, Phoenix Theatre (Dir.: Peter Brook)

FILM

1955

Philip of Spain in *That Lady* (Dir. : Terence Young)